Centers for Disease Control and Prevention

Morbidity and Mortality Weekly Report

Surveillance Summaries / Vol. 60 / No. 5

May 6, 2011

Surveillance for Traumatic Brain Injury–Related Deaths — United States, 1997–2007

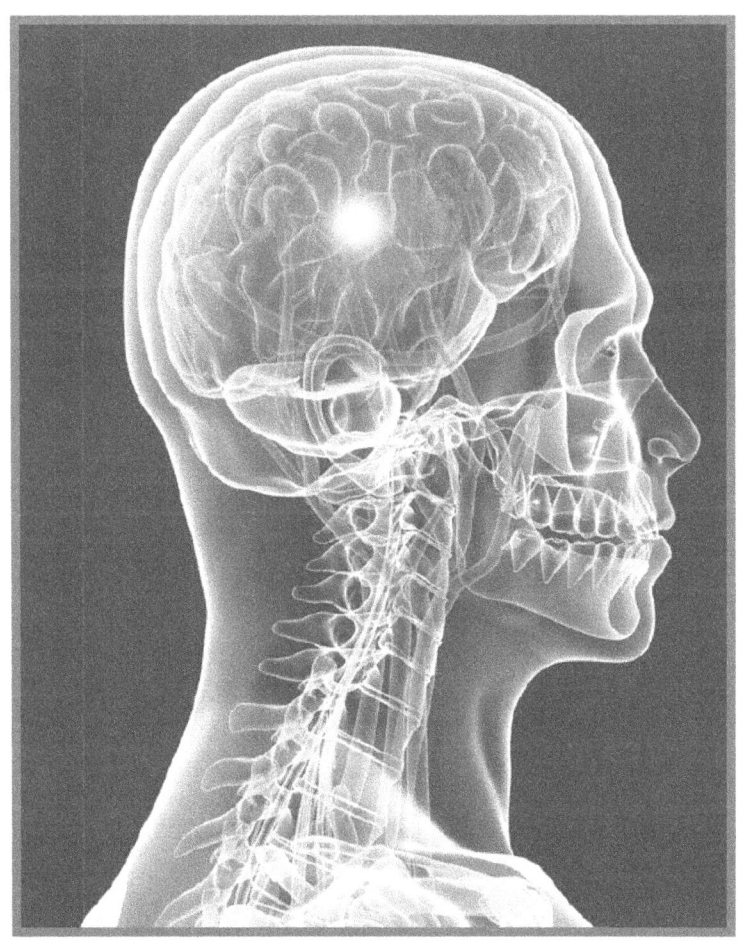

U.S. Department of Health and Human Services
Centers for Disease Control and Prevention

CONTENTS

The *MMWR* series of publications is published by the Office of Surveillance, Epidemiology, and Laboratory Services, Centers for Disease Control and Prevention (CDC), U.S. Department of Health and Human Services, Atlanta, GA 30333.

Suggested Citation: Centers for Disease Control and Prevention. [Title]. MMWR 2011;60(No. SS-#):[inclusive page numbers].

Surveillance for Traumatic Brain Injury–Related Deaths — United States, 1997–2007

Victor G. Coronado, MD[1]
Likang Xu, MD[1]
Sridhar V. Basavaraju, MD[1]
Lisa C. McGuire, PhD[1]
Marlena M. Wald, MPH[1]
Mark D. Faul, PhD[1]
Bernardo R. Guzman, MD[2]
John D. Hemphill[1]

[1]*Division of Injury Response, National Center for Injury Prevention and Control, CDC, Atlanta, Georgia*
[2]*Preventive Medicine and Public Health Residency Program, Andalusian Preventive Medicine and Public Health Training Unit, Spain*

Abstract

Problem/Condition: Traumatic brain injury (TBI) is a leading cause of death and disability in the United States. Approximately 53,000 persons die from TBI-related injuries annually. During 1989–1998, TBI-related death rates decreased 11.4%, from 21.9 to 19.4 per 100,000 population. This report describes the epidemiology and annual rates of TBI-related deaths during 1997–2007.

Reporting Period: January 1, 1997–December 31, 2007.

Description of System: Data were analyzed from the CDC multiple-cause-of-death public-use data files, which contain death certificate data from all 50 states and the District of Columbia.

Results: During 1997–2007, an annual average of 53,014 deaths (18.4 per 100,000 population; range: 17.8–19.3) among U.S. residents were associated with TBIs. During this period, death rates decreased 8.2%, from 19.3 to 17.8 per 100,000 population (p = 0.001). TBI-related death rates decreased significantly among persons aged 0–44 years and increased significantly among those aged ≥75 years. The rate of TBI deaths was three times higher among males (28.8 per 100,000 population) than among females (9.1). Among males, rates were highest among non-Hispanic American Indian/Alaska Natives (41.3 per 100,000 population) and lowest among Hispanics (22.7). Firearm- (34.8%), motor-vehicle– (31.4%), and fall-related TBIs (16.7%) were the leading causes of TBI-related death. Firearm-related death rates were highest among persons aged 15–34 years (8.5 per 100,000 population) and ≥75 years (10.5). Motor vehicle–related death rates were highest among those aged 15–24 years (11.9 per 100,000 population). Fall-related death rates were highest among adults aged ≥75 years (29.8 per 100,000 population). Overall, the rates for all causes except falls decreased.

Interpretation: Although the overall rate of TBI-related deaths decreased during 1997–2007, TBI remains a public health problem; approximately 580,000 persons died with TBI-related diagnoses during this reporting period in the United States. Rates of TBI-related deaths were higher among young and older adults and certain minority populations. The leading external causes of this condition were incidents related to firearms, motor vehicle traffic, and falls.

Public Health Actions: Accurate, timely, and comprehensive surveillance data are necessary to better understand and prevent TBI-related deaths in the United States. CDC multiple-cause-of-death public-use data files can be used to monitor the incidence of TBI-related deaths and assist public health practitioners and partners in the development, implementation, and evaluation of programs and policies to reduce and prevent TBI-related deaths in the United States. Rates of TBI-related deaths are higher in certain population groups and are primarily related to specific external causes. Better enforcement of existing seat belt laws, implementation and increased coverage of more stringent helmet laws, and the implementation of existing evidence-based fall-related prevention interventions are examples of interventions that can reduce the incidence of TBI in the United States.

Introduction

Traumatic brain injury (TBI) is a leading cause of injury death and disability in the United States, and persons of all ages, races/ethnicities, and incomes are affected (*1*). During 2002–2006, on average, approximately 1.7 million U.S. civilians sustained a

Corresponding author: Victor G. Coronado, MD, National Center for Injury Prevention and Control, CDC, 4770 Buford Highway, MS F-62, Atlanta, GA 30341. Telephone: 770-488-1568; Fax: 770-488-3551; E-mail: vgc1@cdc.gov.

TBI annually; of these, approximately 1.4 million were treated and released from emergency departments (EDs), 275,000 were hospitalized and discharged alive, and 52,000 died (2). TBI-related deaths represent approximately one third of all injury-related deaths (3). These deaths do not include persons who had a TBI while serving abroad in the U.S. military and those who did not seek medical care. Certain estimates suggest that persons who did not seek care might account for one fourth of all persons who sustain a TBI in the United States (4).

Overall in the United States, the highest combined rates of TBI-related ED visits, hospitalizations, and deaths occur in young children (aged <5 years), followed by adolescents (aged 15–19 years) and adults aged ≥75 years (2). Overall, males account for approximately 59% of all reported TBI cases in the United States (2). Older adults have the highest rates of TBI hospitalizations and deaths among all age groups (2), and TBI is the leading cause of injury-related death in children and young adults in the United States and other industrialized countries (5). The leading causes of TBI in the U.S. civilian population are falls (35%), motor vehicle–related injuries (17%), and a strike or blow to the head from or against an object (e.g., workplace or sports-related injuries [16.5%], assaults [10%], and other and unknown causes [21%] [2]). The incidence of blast-induced TBI in U.S. civilian populations is low, with a report of 0.2% of TBI cases in a major urban trauma center (6).

A comparison of rates over time reveals an increase in the incidence of TBI-related ED visits and hospitalizations during 1995–2006 (2,7). During that period, the age-adjusted rates of TBI-related ED visits increased from 401 to 468 per 100,000 population, and hospitalizations increased from 86 to 94 per 100,000 population. Meanwhile, deaths decreased from 18.1 to 17.4 per 100,000 population (2,7), a decrease that likely is attributable to preventive measures, such as seat belt use (8), helmet use (9,10), and better overall treatment for severe TBI in prehospital and hospital settings (11).

Long-term TBI-related disability results in reduced quality of life for the patient and prolonged medical, social, and economic effects on society (1,12–15). Current estimates suggest that approximately 3.2–5.3 million persons (1.1%–1.7% of the U.S. population) live with long-term disabilities (the loss of one or more physical or mental functions, such as fine motor skills needed to type) that result from an injury to the brain (16–18). These are likely underestimates of the prevalence of TBI because they do not include persons with TBI sequelae who were treated and released from EDs, those who sought care in other health-care settings, and those who did not seek treatment. The annual economic cost of TBI in the United States, including direct medical and rehabilitation costs and indirect societal economic costs, is estimated to be $60 billion (15).

Using vital statistics data for 1997–2007, this report provides the most recent estimates of TBI-related deaths in the United States. Also described are the leading external causes of death; the risk for TBI-related death by age, sex, race, and intention; and the populations at greatest risk for TBI-related death.

Methods

Data Source and Study Period

Data from the CDC multiple-cause-of-death public use data files (19) were analyzed for January 1, 1997–December 31, 2007. Records analyzed in this study encompass parts I and II of the cause of death section of the death certificate and reflect the data originally reported by the reporting official who completed the death certificate. These data were compiled from death certificates submitted from the vital records offices of all 50 states and the District of Columbia (DC) and include deaths among veterans and active members of the Armed Forces that occurred within the 50 states and DC. Deaths that occurred outside the United States among U.S. residents and members of the Armed Forces are not included (http://www.cdc.gov/nchs/data_access/cmf.htm). The causes of death were recorded on the death certificate by the attending physician, medical examiner, or coroner using a format specified by the World Health Organization in collaboration with CDC (20). This report on TBI-related deaths includes *International Classification of Diseases, Ninth Revision* (ICD-9) coded data for 1997 and 1998 and *International Classification of Diseases, Tenth Revision* (ICD-10) coded data for 1999–2007 to highlight the impact of the ICD-10 implementation in 1999; the results of a bridge-coding study between these revisions are included and discussed briefly.

Case Definition

Cases of TBI were identified and selected from parts I and II of the death certificates in which one or more diagnostic codes representing TBI (21,22) were included in the sequence of conditions contributing to death. The following ICD-9 diagnosis codes were used to identify TBI deaths for 1997–1998 (22,23) in mortality data:
- 800: fracture of vault of skull;
- 801: fracture of base of skull;
- 803: other skull fracture;
- 804: multiple fractures involving skull or face with other bones;
- 850: concussion;
- 851: cerebral laceration and contusion;
- 852: subdural, subarachnoid, and extradural hemorrhage after injury;

- 853: other unspecified intracranial hemorrhage after injury;
- 854: intracranial injury, not otherwise specified;
- 905.0: late effects of fracture of the skull and face;
- 907.0: late effects of intracranial injury without skull fracture; and
- 873: other open wound to the head.

The following ICD-10 nature-of-injury codes were used to identify TBI deaths in mortality data for 1999–2007 (2):

- S01.0–S01.9: open wound of the head;
- S02.0, S02.1, S02.3, S02.7–S02.9: fracture of the skull and facial bones;
- S04.0: injury to optic nerve and pathways;
- S06.0–S06.9: intracranial injury;
- S07.0, S07.1, S07.8, S07.9: crushing injury of head;
- S09.7–S09.9: other and unspecified injuries of head;
- T01.0: open wounds involving head with neck;
- T02.0: fractures involving head with neck;
- T04.0: crushing injuries involving head with neck;
- T06.0: injuries of brain and cranial nerve with injuries of nerves and spinal cord at neck level; and
- T90.1, T90.2, T90.4, T90.5, T90.8, T90.9: sequelae of injuries of head.

To address technical issues related to the implementation of ICD-10, CDC conducted a study in which all cases of TBI-related deaths for 1996 were coded using both ICD-9 and ICD-10 codes (24). The results of this study indicate that the agreement between the ICD-9 and ICD-10 codes used to identify TBI is nearly 96.5%, with a comparability ratio of 0.9985 (24,25). The term agreement indicates that a record is classified in the same ICD category (e.g., TBI) regardless of which ICD revision is used to classify the record. The percentage of agreement reflects the proportion of records that were classified as TBI related both using ICD-9 and ICD-10 coding among all records classified as TBI related. The comparability ratio is calculated by dividing the number of records classified as TBI related when coded using ICD-10 divided by the number of records classified as TBI related when coded using ICD-9, regardless of whether these are the same records. The comparability ratio better describes the impact that ICD-10 implementation had on cause-specific statistical trends. A comparability ratio of 1.00 implies that the number classified as TBI related is virtually unchanged using ICD-10 coding compared with ICD-9 coding.

For this report, the external causes of death were obtained from the underlying cause-of-death field of the mortality file. External cause-of-injury categories for 1997–1998 are based on ICD-9 codes and for 1999–2007 are based on ICD-10 codes (25). However, the ICD-9 and ICD-10 codes are different. For example, in the ICD-9 version, the prefix used to distinguish external causes begins with an E, whereas in ICD-10, the prefix begins with V, W, X, Y, or U. In addition, the organization-of-transport incident codes are different. These codes are based on type of vehicle and the characteristics of the injured person in ICD-9 and ICD-10, respectively. The ICD-9 and ICD-10 coding study conducted by CDC using 1996 data indicated that the overall comparability ratio for all causes of injury combined was relatively good (1.0159); similarly good were the ratios for unintentional and undetermined falls (0.9991 and 0.9857, respectively) and assaults (1.0020, including firearm and other). In contrast, the comparability ratio for unintentional motor vehicle traffic–related TBI was poor (0.9545). The comparability ratios varied by specific external mechanism of death (i.e., for motorcycles, 1.1520; for pedestrian, 0.9535; for pedal cycle, 0.8038; for occupant, 0.6191) and was not determined for other and unspecified causes (24,25).

Given the overall comparability ratios for both nature of injury and external causes of death, no adjustments were made to the trend data presented in this report. Similarly, because averaged data presented in this report involved 2 years of data with ICD-9 codes and 9 years of data with ICD-10 codes, the impact of implementing ICD-10 might somewhat be negligible, and no adjustments were made.

For injuries, ICD-9 (23) and ICD-10 (26) specify that the underlying cause should be coded and that the nature-of-injury codes alone cannot be used to classify underlying cause of death. Therefore, as in a previous CDC report (27), the suffix "related" was added to describe TBI external causes (e.g., motor vehicle–related TBI death). The underlying cause of death is defined as 1) the disease or injury that initiated the chain of health-related events leading directly to death or 2) the circumstances of the accident or violence that produced the fatal injury (23). For all deaths, the underlying cause is selected from conditions reported in the medical certification section of the death certificate. The method used in this report identifies more TBIs than the method used in previous CDC reports (2,7).

Stratifying and Calculating Rates

Data were stratified by age, race, sex, and external cause. Age groups (i.e., 0–4, 5–9, 10–14, 15–19, 20–24, 25–34, 35–44, 45–54, 55–64, 65–74, 75–84, and ≥85 years) are based on a previous CDC publication (2). Age-adjusted rates were standardized to the U.S. census population estimates for 2000 by the direct method (2). To more precisely calculate age-adjusted and age-specific rates, 342 cases with missing age data were excluded. However, excluded cases were included in the calculation of crude rates. Specific TBI fatality rates for three race categories with the highest incidence of TBI (i.e., black,

American Indian/Alaska Native [AI/AN], and white) and for Hispanic ethnicity were calculated, as were sex- and age-specific rates. Because race and Hispanic origin are reported separately on death certificates, persons can be classified as Hispanic or non-Hispanic, and persons of Hispanic origin might be of any race. In this report, data for Hispanics were not calculated separately by race but were classified as Hispanic. Data for non-Hispanic persons were tabulated by race; therefore, in this report, blacks, AI/ANs, and whites are all non-Hispanic. These race/ethnicity-related rates were based on U.S. bridged-race population estimates of the resident population released and maintained by CDC for individual years (28). Bridged-race estimates permit estimation and comparison of race-specific statistics at a point in time or over time (28). Data for Hispanic origin should be interpreted with caution because of inconsistencies between reporting Hispanic origin on death certificates and on censuses and surveys. External causes of TBI deaths were categorized on the basis of CDC-recommended ICD-9 and ICD-10 external cause-of-injury codes (Table 1). Other causes of TBI-related deaths that are intentional (e.g., child maltreatment and interpersonal violence) and unintentional (e.g., sport and recreational injuries) are not addressed in this report. Numbers, rates, and 95% confidence intervals (95% CIs) were calculated before rounding and determined based on the totals for all 11 years, not the annual average; therefore, certain results might not be consistent among the report tables. Appropriate 95% CIs were calculated for all rates presented in this report on the basis of standard errors for random variation in the number of deaths each year, as recommended by CDC (29). Rates calculated from a sample size of <20 for all years combined are not shown because they are unstable (2). Linear regression was used to determine the significance of change over time during the interval and the decrease of specific external causes of death (i.e., motor vehicle–related, firearm-related, and fall-related TBIs). Differences with p values <0.05 were considered statistically significant.

Results

During 1997–2007, an annual average of 53,014 TBI-related deaths (18.4 per 100,000 population; range: 50,680–54,906) occurred among U.S. residents (Table 2). During this period, deaths decreased 8.2%, from 19.3 to 17.8 per 100,000 population (p = 0.001).

Age Group

The TBI-related mortality rate for 1997–2007 was highest among persons aged ≥75 years, especially those aged ≥85 years (Figure 1). During this period, overall TBI-death rates decreased significantly among persons aged 0–44 years (p = 0.002), especially among those aged 5–19 years (p<0.001), and increased significantly among those aged ≥75 years (p = 0.03) (Table 3). TBI-related death rates remained relatively unchanged among persons aged 45–74 years.

Sex

The TBI-related mortality rate for males decreased from 30.5 per 100,000 population in 1997 to 27.9 in 2007 (8.5%; p = 0.002). Among females, this rate decreased by 9.5%, from 9.6 to 8.7 per 100,000 population (p<0.001) (Table 2). During each year of this reporting period, the TBI-related death rates among males in each age and race group were higher than those among females, especially among persons aged 20–24 years. In this age group, males had rates at least four times higher than those for females (Table 3).

Race/Ethnicity

Overall and for males and females, AI/ANs had the highest annual average TBI-related death rates (27.3; 41.3 and 14.4 per 100,000 population, respectively) (Table 2 and Figure 2). Blacks had the second-highest annual average rates of TBI-related deaths overall (19.3 per 100,000 population) and for males (32.2 per 100,000 population) (Table 2). Hispanics had the lowest rates of TBI deaths overall and for both males and females (14.4; 22.7 and 6.3 per 100,000 population, respectively) (Table 2 and Figure 2). During this reporting period, the annual TBI-related death rates decreased for all racial/ethnic groups, especially for AI/ANs (p = 0.002) and blacks (p<0.001). The TBI-related death rates by sex decreased significantly among black males (p<0.001) and females (p<0.001) and AI/AN females (p<0.001). These rates also decreased significantly among Hispanic males (p<0.001) (Table 2).

Mechanisms of TBI-Related Deaths

During 1997–2007, firearm-related events (34.8%), motor vehicle–related events (31.4%), and fall-related events (16.7%) were the leading causes of TBI-related death (Figures 3 and 4). TBI-related death rates varied by sex and age group (Table 4 and Figure 5). Firearm-related TBI death rates were highest among persons aged 20–24 and ≥75 years. Motor vehicle–related TBI death rates were highest among persons aged 15–24 years. Fall-related TBI death rates were highest among adults aged ≥75 years and increased significantly with age. In each age group and for each external cause, males had higher rates of TBI-related death than females (Table 4).

During 1997–2007, the rates of fall-related TBI deaths increased by 59.6%, from 2.4 to 3.8 per 100,000 population (p<0.001) (Table 5 and Figure 4); during the same period, the rates for firearm-related TBI deaths decreased by 13.6%, from 7.2 to 6.2 per 100,000 population (p = 0.004) (Table 6 and Figure 4), and the rates of motor vehicle–related TBI deaths decreased by 22.0%, from 6.4 to 5.0 per 100,000 population (p<0.001) (Table 7 and Figure 4). The observed increases and decreases by each external mechanism occurred almost at a constant rate each year during the reporting period (Tables 5–7 and Figure 4).

Firearms

During 1997–2007, rates of firearm-related TBI death were higher in males, with the highest rates among persons aged 20–24 and ≥75 years (Table 4). Overall, the rates among males (11.2 per 100,000 population) were approximately 6 times higher than among females (1.8 per 100,000 population) (Table 4). Among all firearm-related TBI deaths, 74.2% were suicides, 22.2% were homicides (Table 6), and 3.6% were unintentional, of unknown intentionality, or related to legal intervention (i.e., injury or poisoning caused by police or other legal authorities, including security guards, during law enforcement activities). In this period, death rates for firearm-related TBI suicides decreased 11.5%, from 5.1 to 4.7 per 100,000 population (p = 0.003), and for firearm-related homicides decreased 21.8%, from 1.7 to 1.4 per 100,000 population (p = 0.03).

During this reporting period, rates of firearm-related TBI death varied by race/ethnicity (Tables 6 and 8). Among blacks (7.6 per 100,000 population), 66.1% were homicides (Table 6); black men aged 20–24 and 25–34 years had the highest annual average rate of firearm-related TBI deaths (43.6 and 28.8 per 100,000 population, respectively) (Table 8). These overall rates among blacks decreased by 22.8%, from 9.3 to 7.2 per 100,000 population (p = 0.02) (Table 6). Whites had the second highest rates of firearm-related TBI deaths (6.5 per 100,000 population) (Table 6). Except among children aged 5–9 years, these rates among white males were higher than among females and increased with age, from 9.1 per 100,000 population among those aged 15–19 years to 34.7 per 100,000 among persons aged ≥85 years (Table 8). In this reporting period, firearm-related TBI deaths among whites decreased slightly until 1999 and remained relatively unchanged since then (Table 6). During 1997–2007, the rates of firearm-related TBI deaths among AI/AN was 6.3 per 100,000 population (Table 6), with 67.5% from suicide (Table 6). These rates were especially high among AI/AN males aged 15–19, 20–24, and 25–34 years (18.6, 25.2, and 18.3 per 100,000 population, respectively) (Table 8). During 1997–2007, firearm-related TBI deaths among AI/ANs remained relatively unchanged (p = 0.1) (Table 6). Hispanics had the lowest annual average rates of firearm-related TBI deaths (3.9 per 100,000 population) (Table 6). These rates were higher among Hispanics

aged 15–19, 20–24, 75–84, and ≥85 years (7.1, 9.1, 4.6, and 4.9 per 100,000 population, respectively) (Table 8). In this reporting period, firearm-related TBI deaths among Hispanics decreased 23.1%, from 4.8 to 3.7 per 100,000 population (p<0.001) (Table 6). Among all race/ethnic and age groups, firearm-related TBI suicides were higher among males than among females; these rates among males were substantially higher among AI/ANs aged 15–34 years and among white men aged ≥65 years. During 1997–2007, the rates of firearm-related TBI homicides were higher among males regardless of race/ethnicity and age group (except among women aged 75–84 years); however, these rates were highest among blacks aged 15–34 years.

Motor Vehicles

During 1997–2007, the overall rate of motor vehicle–related TBI deaths among males (8.2 per 100,000 population) was 2.4 times higher than among females (3.5 per 100,000 population) (Table 4). This rate was also higher among males in every age group. The highest rates were among males aged 15–19 years (15.3 per 100,000 population), 20–24 years (17.9 per 100,000 population), and ≥85 years (13.0 per 100,000 population) (Table 4).

During this reporting period, rates of motor vehicle–related TBI deaths varied by race (Tables 7 and 9). AI/ANs had the highest annual average rate of motor vehicle–related TBI deaths (11.5 per 100,000 population) (Table 7). The rate among AI/ANs decreased significantly by 24.5%, from 12.8 per 100,000 population in 1997 to 9.5 per 100,000 population in 2007 (p = 0.001) (Table 7). Whites had the second-highest annual average rate of motor vehicle–related TBI deaths (6.1 per 100,000 population) (Table 7), decreasing 20.1%, from 6.7 per 100,000 population in 1997 to 5.3 per 100,000 population in 2007 (p<0.001) (Table 7). In addition, blacks (5.4 per 100,000 population) and Hispanics (5.0 per 100,000 population) had the lowest average annual rates of motor vehicle–related TBI deaths (Table 7). These rates among blacks decreased 27.2% (p<0.001), from 6.2 to 4.5 per 100,000 population, and among Hispanics decreased 22.4% (p = 0.03), from 5.4 to 4.2 per 100,000 population during 1997–2007 (Table 7). Overall, in each racial group, and in both sexes (except AI/AN girls aged 5–14 years), rates of motor vehicle–related TBI death rates were highest among males, especially among those aged 15–24 years (Table 9). In each racial group, these rates increased with age for those aged 65–84 years. However, among white males, these age-related increases also occurred among persons aged ≥85 years (Table 9).

During 1997–2007, the annual overall rates of motor vehicle–related TBI deaths decreased significantly among vehicle occupants by 45.5%, from 3.7 to 2.0 per 100,000 population (p<0.001); among pedestrians by 32.8%, from 0.8 to 0.5 per 100,000 population (p<0.001); and among pedal cyclists by

49.4%, from 0.2 to 0.1 per 100,000 population (p = 0.02) (Table 10). In contrast, motorcycle-related TBI death rates for the same period increased 133.1%, from 0.3 to 0.6 per 100,000 population (p<0.001) (Table 10). During this period, rates decreased significantly among vehicle occupants, pedal cyclists, and pedestrians of all racial/ethnic groups except AI/AN pedal cyclists (Tables 11 and 12). In contrast, the rates of TBI-related deaths among motorcyclists of all racial/ethnic groups significantly increased in this reporting period (p<0.001; Tables 10–12).

Falls

The overall rate of fall-related TBI deaths among males (3.7 per 100,000 population) was 1.5 times higher than among females (2.5 per 100,000 population) during this reporting period (Table 13). These rates in all age groups were also higher among males than females and increased significantly with age for both sexes. Overall, the highest rates of fall-related TBI deaths were among men aged 65–74 years (9.4 per 100,000 population), 75–84 years (29.2 per 100,000 population), and ≥85 years (78.4 per 100,000 population) (Tables 4 and 13). Similarly, the highest rates of fall-related TBI deaths were among females aged 65–74 years (4.5 per 100,000 population), 75–84 years (16.0 per 100,000 population), and ≥85 years (43.4 per 100,000 population) (Tables 4 and 13). Compared with overall annual rates of fall-related TBI deaths for persons aged 55–64 years, the rate ratio was 2.2 for persons aged 65–74 years, 7.1 for persons aged 75–84 years, and 17.8 for persons aged ≥85 years.

During 1997–2007, rates of fall-related TBI deaths varied by race/ethnicity (Table 13). AI/ANs had the highest annual average rate of fall-related TBI deaths (3.6 per 100,000 population) (Table 5), with the rate increasing 24.7% (p = 0.02), from 3.4 to 4.2 per 100,000 population (Table 5). Whites had the second-highest annual average rate of fall-related TBI deaths (3.2 per 100,000 population) (Table 5). This rate increased significantly by 67.2% (p<0.001), from 2.4 to 4.0 per 100,000 population (Table 5). The third-highest annual average rate of fall-related TBI deaths was among Hispanics (2.7 per 100,000 population) and blacks (2.0 per 100,000 population) (Table 5), with rates increasing 32.7% (p<0.001) during 1997–2007, from 2.2 to 3.0 per 100,000 population, and 17.1% (p = 0.02), from 1.8 to 2.1 per 100,000 population, respectively (Table 5). Overall and in each racial group, except among those aged 5–9 years, rates of fall-related TBI deaths were highest among males, particularly among those aged ≥65 years (Table 13).

Places of TBI-Related Deaths

During 1997–2007, the most common places of death related to TBI were inpatient facilities (5.3 per 100,000 population) and homes (4.1 per 100,000 population). Rates of TBI-related deaths in other and unknown places were 5.5 per 100,000 population (Table 14). The annual rates of TBI deaths during 1997–2007 decreased 59.4% for those who died on arrival, from 1.0 to 0.4 per 100,000 population (p<0.001), and 21.7% among those seen in EDs and other outpatient facilities, from 2.5 to 1.9 per 100,000 population (p<0.001) (Table 14). In contrast, during 1997–2007, these rates remained relatively stable in nursing homes (p = 0.69) and inpatient facilities (p = 0.67) (Table 14). During this period, AI/ANs and blacks had the highest overall average annual rate of TBI deaths occurring in inpatient settings, in EDs and other outpatient facilities, and among those who were dead on arrival. The rates among those who died in nursing homes and at home were higher among AI/ANs and whites (Table 15).

Discussion

The data presented in this report document an overall 8.2% decrease, from 19.3 to 17.8 per 100,000 population, in rates of TBI-related death in the United States during 1997–2007. Although less steep than in previous reporting periods, these trends follow the decreases reported by CDC for 1979–1992, from 24.6 to 19.3 per 100,000 population (30), and 1989–1998, from 21.9 to 19.4 per 100,000 population (27). During the current reporting period and during 1989–1998 (27), firearms continued to exceed motor vehicle crashes as the largest single mechanism of TBI-related death in the United States. Fall-related TBI deaths (especially among older adults) continued to increase, offsetting some of the decreases observed in motor vehicle–related and firearm-related TBI death rates during these periods. Overall, the rates of TBI-related deaths decreased slightly during this reporting period. This decrease highlights the successful efforts to prevent TBIs related to motor vehicle crashes. Given the substantially high rates, additional improvements are warranted targeting prevention of TBI deaths from falls and firearms

Multiple factors might have contributed to the overall decreases in TBI-related deaths. The largest decreases observed since the 1980s might be related to a decrease in motor vehicle–related deaths, largely because of the widespread use of seat belts, airbags, child safety seats, and motorcycle helmets (31–33). Other contributing factors to the observed decreases in motor vehicle–related TBI deaths include graduated licensing of novice, young drivers; education programs to improve driver performance and safety (1,34,35); and changes to public policy and safety laws, including reduction of speed limits, seat belt and helmet laws, and road engineering practices (36). In addition, improved prehospital triage and referral, care of injured persons, and improved emergency and neurotrauma services in hospitals might also have helped to reduce the rate of TBI deaths (*37–43*).

Fall-related TBI death rates have steadily increased since the 1990s (*27,30*), especially among those aged ≥65 years. The results of this report indicate that rates of fatal fall-related TBI among those aged ≥65 years substantially increased with increasing age. These increases might partially be a result of improved diagnostic imaging, which allows for enhanced identification of TBI (*43*), better reporting (*27*), or the increasing occurrence of other age-related factors that predispose persons to falling and fall-related TBI (*44*). Examples of associated intrinsic factors include relevant health conditions (e.g., diabetes mellitus, cardiac arrhythmias, or blood dyscrasias); impaired balance; slower reaction times; decreased muscular strength; impaired cognition; use of multiple medications that might cause dizziness, postural hypotension, impaired reflexes and judgment; or use of anticoagulants (*27,44–52*). Extrinsic factors might also contribute to increased fall risk among older adults. These include living alone or in dwellings with clutter, poorly lighted spaces, or slippery surfaces and in dwellings with no safety features in bathrooms or on stairs (*27,44,53–59*). As the proportion of older adults continues to increase in the United States (*60,61*), more efficient and cost-effective fall-related prevention interventions must be designed and widely adopted especially in homes, health-care settings, and long-term care facilities (*44*). Because the ICD-9 to ICD-10 comparability ratio for fall-related in injuries is close to 1, changes in coding had minimal impact on these statistics.

Firearms

Firearm-related injuries are the second leading mechanism of injury death in the United States (*62*). Since 2000, approximately 30,000 persons have died each year from firearm-related injuries (*63*). Firearm-related head injuries are especially lethal; approximately two thirds of these injuries result in death (*64*). Approximately 75% of intentionally self-inflicted and 40% of firearm-related assault injury deaths result from injuries to the brain (*64*). Although the rates of firearm-related TBI deaths decreased during 1997–2007, males continued to have statistically significantly higher rates of death than females. The circumstances of the deaths in these groups might be attributed to homicide, suicide, and unintentional injury or other causes. Identification of the particular groups that are at risk provides opportunities for targeted prevention efforts.

The substantial number of boys aged 10–14 years who died from a TBI-related firearm injury suggests the potential for public health prevention measures. Interventions to reduce the risk for firearm-related deaths or injuries can be behavior oriented (e.g., education regarding safe storage and handling of guns, modification of other identifiable risk factors, and counseling) (*65,66*), product oriented (e.g., changing the design of firearms or making them more difficult for children or others to use unintentionally or intentionally if stolen or obtained illegally) (*67*), or policy oriented (e.g., licensing requirements and gun storage laws) (*68–70*). Because these measures have not been adequately evaluated, it is difficult to know which are the most effective in reducing firearm-related deaths or injuries (*71*). Continued targeted public health efforts and promotion of safe storage of firearms in households with children or households frequently visited by children is warranted.

Implementation of evidence-based strategies for the primary prevention of violence also is needed to reduce risk for homicide among adolescents and young adults. A substantial amount of research has identified risk factors for violence and weapon carrying and prevention strategies. For example, the *Blueprints for Violence Prevention* has identified 11 model programs and 19 promising programs that have shown significant, sustained reductions on youth violence or risk factors for youth violence (*72*). The substantial rate of firearm-related TBI suicide among older adults calls for improved screening for signs and symptoms of suicide, access to mental health care, and prevention strategies designed for this population. In 2004, persons aged ≥65 years comprised 12% of the U.S. population but accounted for 16% of suicide deaths (*73*). In addition, in 2004, the rate of suicide among persons aged ≥65 years was 14.3 per 100,000 population, compared with 11 per 100,000 in the general population (*73*). Previously, comorbid conditions including depression, mood disorders, and cancer have been associated with suicide among older adults (*74*). In addition, older adults who commit suicide are more likely to live in lower per capita income areas than persons in other age groups (*75*). Strategies that might be implemented to prevent firearm-related TBI suicides among older adults include health policy measures and population-based interventions to improve mental health care access in lower socioeconomic areas (*76*). An additional strategy to prevent suicidal behavior in all age and racial/ethnic groups includes building and strengthening individual, family, and community connectedness (http://www.cdc.gov/violenceprevention/pdf/suicide_strategic_direction_full_version-a.pdf).

Motor Vehicles

Of the 53,014 TBI-related deaths that occur on average each year in the United States, motor vehicle–related incidents are the second leading cause (31.4%). Although these data highlight the substantial role of motor vehicle–related events in TBI deaths, during 1997–2007, motor vehicle–related TBI deaths decreased 22.0%, from 6.4 to 5.0 per 100,000 population. This decrease paralleled the 9.5% reduction in overall motor vehicle–related deaths monitored by the National Highway Transportation Safety Administration (NHTSA) for 1995–2006 (77). These results indicated a decrease from 15.9 to 14.2 per 100,000 population, although vehicle miles traveled increased 21.4% from 2.5 billion to 3.0 billion during this period (77). The rate of motor vehicle crash deaths per 100 million miles traveled by drivers also decreased significantly by 62.7%, from 3.4 in 1975 to 1.3 in 2008 (78). One of the major factors in the decrease in motor vehicle–related deaths, including those with a TBI-related diagnosis, has been increased seat belt use supported by primary and secondary enforcement legislation. Under the primary legislation, a motorist can be stopped and ticketed solely on the basis on not wearing a seat belt; as of May 2009, 26 states and DC had such laws (79). Under secondary legislation, a motorist must be stopped for another violation before the person can be cited for not using a seat belt; as of May 2010, a total of 19 states had such laws (79). A 2009 CDC study using data from the Behavioral Risk Factor Surveillance System (BRFSS) found that the median adult seat belt use in the United States and U.S. territories was 82.4% (range: 58.3% in North Dakota and South Dakota to 91.9% in California) (80). On average, seat belt use was 10.1 percentage points higher in states and territories with primary enforcement laws (86.0%) than in states with secondary enforcement laws (75.9%) (80). Furthermore, primary enforcement laws seem to have the greatest effect on sociodemographic groups that traditionally report lower levels of seat belt use (e.g., persons with less than a high school education, with an annual household income <$20,000, or who live in rural areas) (81).

However, even promulgation of such laws does not result in all adults using seat belts regularly, even when children are in the vehicle. A CDC study of approximately 9,000 adult drivers indicated that 15.9% of these drivers with at least one child in their household did not always wear a seat belt when driving with a child or children from their household (82). In addition, 17.5% of the adults interviewed did not wear seat belts when traveling as passengers with a child or children from their household (82). Lack of appropriate child safety restraint plays a role in deaths as well. In 2006, NHTSA reported that 1,794 vehicle occupants aged ≤14 years were involved in fatal crashes; among those whose restraint status was known, 25% were unrestrained (83).

Additional contributing factors to pediatric motor vehicle crash deaths include adult drivers who drive with a child or children from their household while under the influence of alcohol (84,85). For example, in 2006, NHTSA reported that of the children aged ≤14 years who were killed in motor vehicle crashes that year, 17% were passengers in vehicles driven by an adult with a blood alcohol concentration (BAC) level of ≥0.08

g/dl (86). CDC found that of the 5,555 U.S. child passenger deaths during 1985–1996, 64% occurred while the child was riding with a drinking driver (i.e., a driver with a measurable blood alcohol concentration >2.17 mmol/L or 10 mg/dL) who was old enough to be the parent or caregiver (87). In the same study, nonfatal motor vehicle–related events were analyzed for 1988–1996; an estimated 58,000 of 149,000 child passengers who were nonfatally injured in crashes involving a drinking driver were injured while riding with a drinking driver (87). In addition, data indicate that as the level of alcohol-related impairment increases and the BAC surpasses the U.S. legal BAC limit of 0.08 g/dL among adult drivers, the percentage of appropriate child safety restraint use decreases (87). In 2007, motor vehicle crashes caused approximately 7% of all AI/AN deaths. During 2003–2007, male AI/ANs had death rates that were 2–4 times higher than the rates of other races/ethnicities, with annual rates of approximately 43 deaths per 100,000 population. Furthermore, during 2003–2007, female AI/ANs also had the highest motor vehicle death rates, with approximately 21 deaths per 100,000 population (88). Given the high rate of TBI deaths among occupants of vehicles in the AI/AN populations in this report and a previous CDC investigation (89), additional studies should be considered to examine these causes, including motor vehicle–related events and BAC levels, in relation to deaths among children. In addition, population-specific, appropriate public health interventions should be designed to reduce motor vehicle–related TBI mortality.

In 2006, there were 30 million licensed drivers aged ≥65 years (approximately 15% of all drivers) in the United States, an increase of 18% from 1996 (90). Older adults represented 14% of all vehicle deaths and 19% of all pedestrian deaths in 2006 (91). Rates for both TBI motor vehicle–related deaths described in this report and overall motor vehicle–related deaths are highest among males in both categories (91). As age increases, men in their 70s and 80s are more likely to be involved in fatal crashes than women (91). In addition, older adults who choose not to drive and prefer to walk (91) increase their risk for motor vehicle–related injuries as pedestrians (92). Although trends in traffic deaths among older drivers have decreased in the United States in recent decades (90), additional study is needed to develop and assess primary prevention strategies for this rapidly increasing population.

Motorcyclists also are at risk for TBI-related deaths. Although annual rates of TBI death among motorcyclists are low, the findings in this report indicate that these rates increased significantly by approximately 133.1% during 1997–2007 (p<0.001). NHTSA estimated that the number of deaths per mile traveled on motorcycles in 2007 was approximately 37 times the number of deaths in cars (93). Motorcyclist deaths doubled during 1997–2008. In contrast, passenger vehicle occupant deaths reached a record low in 2008 (*93*).

Among the many factors that might have contributed to the increase in motorcyclist deaths, helmet use and laws seem to play a major role (*94*). Because motorcyclists are more prone to crash injuries than car occupants, wearing a helmet and protective clothing are the primary interventions to reduce injuries, including TBI, which is a leading cause of death among riders who do not wear helmets (*94*). Although a study conducted in the mid 1980s found that helmets might increase the risk for neck injuries (*95*), more recent evidence indicates that helmet use is not associated with increased neck injuries (*96–98*). Implementation of universal helmet laws (i.e., covering all riders) or weakening or repealing such laws might affect motorcycle-related TBI morbidity and mortality. Implementation of a universal helmet use law in California in 1992 increased helmet use to 99% from approximately 50% in 1991 (*99*), and the number of motorcyclist deaths in that state decreased approximately 37% during 1991–1992 (*100*). These data suggest that adequately enforced universal helmet laws can result in high rates of helmet use (*99–101*) and reduce mortality. In contrast, after Florida limited the coverage of its helmet law in 2000, exempting riders aged ≥21 years with ≥$10,000 of medical insurance coverage, NHTSA found that motorcyclist deaths per 10,000 motorcycle registrations increased 21% during the 2 years after the law was changed (*102*). These data suggest that helmet use laws that apply only to selected riders are difficult to enforce (*103*); moreover, these laws might be less effective than universal helmet laws at reducing crash-related deaths and injuries among the youngest drivers (*102,103*). Prevalence of helmet use for all riders remains low (approximately 50%) in states where limited-coverage laws or no helmet laws are in effect (*102,104*), and death rates are 20%–40% higher in states with weak laws or no laws compared with rates in states with helmet laws that apply to all riders (*105*). In 2010, a total of 20 states and DC had universal helmet laws, 27 states had laws covering certain riders (usually persons aged <18 years), and Illinois, Iowa, and New Hampshire did not have helmet laws (*106*).

Falls

Among adults aged ≥65 years, falls are the leading mechanism of injury deaths (*107,108*) and the leading external mechanism of TBI (*2,108*). The findings of this report suggest that the overall annual rates of fall-related TBI deaths increase dramatically with increasing age. Consistent with the increase in the number of older adults in the U.S. population and because persons are living longer, results in this report suggest that the rates of fall-related TBI mortality among older adults

increased significantly during 1997–2007, paralleling the observed increases with age in TBI incidence among older adults (*2,108*).

Each year, approximately one third of older adults fall, and the likelihood of falling increases with advancing age (*108*). Data from the 2006 BRFSS indicated that approximately 5.8 million persons aged ≥65 years, or 15.9% of all U.S. adults in that age group, had fallen at least once during the preceding 3 months (*109*). Of respondents who reported that they had fallen, 23.1% indicated falling three or more times in the preceding 3 months (*110*). Even though older adults fall more frequently than younger persons, falls are not an inevitable consequence of aging (*109*). Fall-related risk factors, including muscle weakness, gait and balance problems, poor vision, use of psychoactive medications, and home hazards (*111*), can be modified to decrease the risk for falls among older adults. Evidenced-based fall-prevention programs already exist to address these modifiable risk factors. The most effective interventions include exercise, either solely or as a component of a multifaceted approach that includes better medication management, vision correction, and home modifications (*44*). More information on evidence-based fall-prevention strategies and other fall-related educational materials are available at http://www.cdc.gov/homeandrecreationalsafety/falls/index-pr.html.

Adult caregivers who care for adults aged ≥18 years are present in three of every 10 households, or approximately 48.9 million caregivers in the United States (21.5% of the U.S. population) (*112*). Because the majority of these caregivers (approximately 34 million) provide care to persons aged ≥50 years (*112–114*), they can help prevent and reduce falls among older adults. Moreover, caregivers help these adults to remain in their community for a longer period (*113,114*). Caregivers can promote healthy living among older adults by learning about TBI prevention measures in the home. *Help Seniors Live Better, Longer: Prevent Brain Injury* is a CDC initiative to raise awareness among caregivers of older adults about ways to prevent, recognize, and respond to TBI. More information is available at http://www.cdc.gov/traumaticbraininjury.

Unless effective preventive measures are implemented, the number of fall-related injuries, including TBI, is likely to increase because the number of persons aged ≥65 years in the United States is expected to increase from almost 35 million in 2000 to 71 million in 2030 (*115*), and the number of persons aged ≥80 years is expected to increase from approximately 9 million in 2000 to 19.5 million in 2030 (*115*). TBIs also might increase in the states with the largest number of older persons (e.g., California, Florida, and Illinois) (*116*) or have the greatest projected increases in these populations. For example, 26% of Florida's population is projected to be aged ≥65 years in 2025 (*117*).

Limitations

The findings in this report are subject to at least four limitations. First, when deaths involve injuries or unusual or suspicious circumstances, the cause of death is typically investigated, certified, and reported by a medical examiner or coroner (*118,119*). In this report, cause-of-death data reported from death certificates rely on accurate reporting and recording by medical examiners and coroners. The number of certificates with inaccurate recording cannot be quantified; therefore, the total number of TBI deaths in this report might be overestimated or underestimated, and cause-of-death data in this report derived from death certificates are subject to incomplete reporting or misclassification. Second, little is known about the accuracy of reported circumstances and causes of injury-related deaths at the national level in the United States. The cause of death for deaths involving an injury tends to be more straightforward than for deaths from other causes because of the immediate fatal outcome; therefore, the accuracy of the reported cause is expected to be high (*120,121*). However, other factors might bias certain causes of death (e.g., lack of specificity regarding the circumstances of the injury [*122,123*] and inconsistencies in the definition and specification of the manner or intent of death [*122*]). Third, depending on the ICD-9 to ICD-10 comparability ratios, implementation of ICD-10 in 1999 might have affected the estimates for selected diagnoses and external cause of injury. Applying the comparability ratios to the ICD-9 portion of the trend does not lead to different conclusions because the ratios that measure the effect of implementing the ICD-10 barely diverge from the null value (1.00). Overall, implementation of ICD-10 had a minimal effect on the TBI-related estimates, as indicated by the good comparability ratio for this condition (*24,25*). However, estimates for selected overall and specific external causes of injury might have increased by as much as 15% for motorcycle-related injuries or decreased by approximately 5% for unintentional motor-vehicle traffic and pedestrians injuries, 20% for pedal cycle-related injuries, and 40% for motor vehicle occupant–related injuries (*24,25*). Nevertheless, during 1999–2007, motorcycle-related TBI deaths increased significantly by 68.3%, and motor-vehicle-related TBI deaths decreased significantly by 22.0. The ICD-9 to ICD-10 comparability ratio for assault-related injuries (including firearms and other) is close to 1, indicating changes in coding had a minimal impact on these estimates. Finally, death rates might have been affected by misclassification of race/ethnicity in both death counts and populations used in rate calculations. CDC has calculated the net effect of underestimating numerators and denominators on death rates by race/ethnicity (*124*). Adjusting for misclassification increases reported numbers of deaths for AI/ANs by 30%, Hispanics by 5%, and blacks by

1%. Adjusting for misclassification also decreases reported rates for blacks by 5% and whites by 1%. Therefore, adjustment for misclassification in this study would have resulted in a slightly decreased difference in rates between blacks and whites and an increased difference in rates between AI/ANs and whites. To allow historical comparisons of TBI-related deaths (*27*), no such adjustments were made in this report.

Conclusion

Although rates of TBI deaths decreased during 1997–2007, an average of approximately 53,000 persons still die annually in the United States with TBI-related diagnoses. In addition, deaths from fall-related TBIs increased, as did rates of firearm-related homicides among persons aged 20–24 years and suicides among persons aged ≥75 years. Although strategies have been developed to prevent and manage falls among older adults (*125*) and to prevent firearm-related suicides and homicides in populations at risk (*126,127*), additional research is needed to identify modifiable risk factors and to develop more effective prevention interventions. A first step toward achieving greater reductions in TBI mortality and morbidity is effective dissemination of findings to persons at high risk for TBI, health care practitioners, public health and injury-control professionals, the public, and policy makers. More information is available at http://www.cdc.gov/traumaticbraininjury.

Acknowledgments

This report is based, in part, on contributions by Arialdi M. Miniño, MPH, Division of Vital Statistics, National Center for Health Statistics, CDC.

References

1. Coronado VG, Thurman DJ, Greenspan AI, Weissman BM. Epidemiology. In: Jallo J, Loftus CM, eds. Neurotrauma and critical care: brain. New York, NY: Thieme; 2009:3–19.
2. Faul M, Xu L, Wald MM, Coronado V. Traumatic brain injury in the United States: emergency department visits, hospitalizations, and deaths, 2002–2006. Atlanta, GA: CDC, National Center for Injury Prevention and Control; 2010.
3. CDC. QuickStats: Injury and traumatic brain injury-related death rates by age—United States, 2006. MMWR 2010;59:303.
4. Sosin DM, Sniezek JE, Thurman DJ. Incidence of mild and moderate brain injury in the United States, 1991. Brain Inj 1996;10:47–54.
5. Babikian T, Asarnow R. Neurocognitive outcomes and recovery after pediatric TBI: meta-analytic review of the literature. Neuropsychology 2009;283–96.
6. Bochicchio GV, Lumpkins K, O'Connor J, et al. Blast injury in a civilian trauma setting is associated with a delay in diagnosis of traumatic brain injury. Am Surg 2008;74:267–70.
7. Langlois JA, Rutland-Brown W, Thomas KE. Traumatic brain injury in the United States: emergency department visits, hospitalizations, and deaths. Atlanta, GA: CDC, National Center for Injury Prevention and Control; 2006.

8. Braver ER, Ferguson SA, Greene MA, Lund AK. Reductions in deaths in frontal crashes among right passengers in vehicles equipped with passenger air bags. JAMA 1997;298:1437–9.

9. Sosin DM, Sacks JJ, Webb KW. Pediatric injuries and deaths from bicycling in the United States. Pediatrics 1996;98:868–70.

10. Thompson RS, Rivara FP, Thompson DC. A case-control study of the effectiveness of bicycle safety helmets. NEJM 1989;320:1361–7.

11. Faul M, Wald M, Rutland Brown W, Sullivent E, Sattin R. Using a cost-benefit analysis to estimate outcomes of a clinical treatment guideline: Testing the Brain Trauma Foundation guidelines for the treatment of severe traumatic brain injury. J Trauma 2007;63:1271–8.

12. Silver JM, Yudofsky SC, Anderson KE. Aggressive disorders. Silver JM, McAllister TW, Yudofsky SC, eds. Textbook of traumatic brain injury. 2nd ed. Washington, DC: American Psychiatric Publishing; 2005:259–77.

13. Kushel MB, Hahn JA, Evans JL, et al. Revolving doors: imprisonment among the homeless and marginally housed population. Am J Public Health 2005;95:1747–52.

14. Brewer Smyth K, Burgess AW, Shults J. Physical and sexual abuse, salivary cortical, and neurologic correlates of violent criminal behavior in female prison inmates. Biological Psychiatry 2004;55:21–31.

15. Finkelstein EA, Corso PS, Miller TR. The incidence and economic burden of injuries in the United States. New York, NY: Oxford University Press; 2006.

16. Zaloshnja E, Miller T, Langlois JA, Selassie AW. Prevalence of long-term disability from traumatic brain injury in the civilian population of the United States, 2005. J Head Trauma Rehab 2008;23:394-400.

17. CDC. Traumatic brain injury in the United States: a report to Congress. Atlanta, GA: US Department of Health and Human Services, CDC; 1999.

18. Selassie AW, Zaloshnja E, Langlois JA, Millet T, Jones P, Steiner C. Incidence of long-term disability following traumatic brain injury hospitalization, United States, 2003. J Head Trauma Rehab 2008;23:123–31.

19. CDC. National Center for Health Statistics multiple cause of death public use data, 1997–2007. Hyattsville, MD: US Department of Health and Human Services, CDC; 2010.

20. CDC. Classification of diseases, functioning, and disability. Hyattsville, MD: CDC, National Center for Health Statistics. Available at http://www.cdc.gov/nchs/icd.htm. Accessed August 1, 2010.

21. Thurman DJ, Sniezek JE, Johnson D, Greenspan A, Smith SM. Guidelines for surveillance of central nervous system injury. Atlanta, GA: US Department of Health and Human Services, Public Health Service, CDC; 1995.

22. Marr A, Coronado VG. Annual data submission standards. Central nervous system injury surveillance. Atlanta, GA: US Department of Health and Human Services, Public Health Service, CDC; 2001.

23. World Health Organization. International classification of diseases: manual on the international statistical classification of diseases, injuries, and cause of death. 9th rev. Geneva, Switzerland: World Health Organization; 1977.

24. Anderson RN, Minino AM, Fingerhut LA, Warner M, Heinen MA. Deaths: injuries 2001. CDC, National Center for Health Statistics: Natl Vital Stat Rep 2004;52(21).

25. Langlois JA, Rutland-Brown W, Thomas KE. Traumatic brain injury in the United States: emergency department visits, hospitalizations, and deaths. Atlanta, GA: CDC, National Center for Injury Prevention and Control; 2004.

26. World Health Organization. International classification of diseases, 10th rev. Geneva, Switzerland: World Health Organization; 2001.

27. CDC. Surveillance for traumatic brain injury deaths—United States, 1989–1998. MMWR 2002;51(No. SS-10).

28. CDC. Bridged-race population estimates: data files and documentation. Hyattsville, MD: CDC, National Center for Health Statistics; 2010. Available at http://www.cdc.gov/nchs/nvss/bridged_race/data_documentation.htm. Accessed February 01, 2010.

29. Hoyert DL, Heron MP, Murphy SL, Kung HC. Deaths: final data for 2003. Natl Vital Stat Rep 2006;54(13).

30. Sosin DM, Sniezek JE, Waxwailer RJ. Trends in deaths associated with traumatic brain injury, 1979 through 1992: success and failure. JAMA 1995;273:1778–80.

31. CDC. Traumatic brain injury. Atlanta, GA: CDC, National Center for Injury Prevention and Control; 2007. Available at http://www.cdc.gov/ncipc/factsheets/tbi.htm. Accessed January 15, 2010.

32. Hardman JM, Manoukian A. Pathology of head trauma. Neuroimag Clin North Am 2002;12:175–87.

33. Liu BC, Ivers R, Norton R, Boufous S, Blows S, Lo SK. Helmets for preventing injury in motorcycle riders [Review]. Cochrane Database Syst Rev 2008;(1):CD004333.

34. CDC. Achievements in public health, 1990–1999 motor vehicle safety: a 20th century public health achievement. MMWR 1999;48:369–74.

35. Zink BJ. Traumatic brain injury outcome: concepts for emergency care. Ann Emerg Med. 2001;37:318–32.

36. Park E, Bell JD, Baker AJ. Traumatic brain injury: can the consequences be stopped? CMAJ 2008;178:1163–70.

37. MacKenzie EJ, Rivara FP, Jurkovich GJ, et al. A national evaluation of the effect of trauma-center care on mortality. NEJM 2006;354:366–78.

38. Mackersie RC. History of trauma field triage development and the American College of Surgeons criteria. Prehosp Emerg Care 2006;10:287–94.

39. CDC. Guidelines for field triage of injured patients. Recommendations of the National Expert Panel on Field Triage. MMWR 2009;58(No. RR-1).

40. Moppett IK. Traumatic brain injury: assessment, resuscitation and early management. Br J Anaesth 2007;99:18–31.

41. Neurotrauma Foundation. Guidelines for the management of severe traumatic brain injury. 3rd ed. J Neurotrauma 2007;24(Supp1):S1–S106.

42. CDC. Injury prevention & control: field triage. Field triage decision scheme. Atlanta, GA: CDC. Available at http://www.cdc.gov/fieldtriage/index.html. Accessed July 26, 2010.

43. Bullock MR, Chesnut RM, Clifton GL, et al. Part I: Guidelines for the management of severe head injury. In: Management and prognosis of severe traumatic brain injury. New York, NY: Brain Trauma Foundation. 2000;7–159.

44. Coronado VG, Thomas KE, Sattin RW, Johnson RL. The CDC traumatic brain injury surveillance system: characteristics of persons aged 65 years and older hospitalized with a TBI. J Head Trauma Rehabil 2005;3:215–28.

45. Kraus JF, McArthur DL. Epidemiologic aspects of brain injury. Neurol Clin 1996;14:435–50.

46. Tinetti ME. Preventing falls in elderly persons. N Engl J Med 2003; 348:42–9.

47. Sasser HC, Hammond FM, Lincourt AE. To fall or not to fall: brain injury in the elderly. N C Med J 2001;62:364–7.

48. Judge JO, Lindsey C. Underwood M, Winsemius D. Balance improvements in older women: effects of exercise training. Phys Ther 1993;73:254–65.

49. Lord SR, Caplan GA, Ward JA. Balance, reaction time, and muscle strength in exercising older women: a pilot study. Arch Phys Med Rehab 1993;74:837–9.

50. Campbell AJ, Robertson MC, Gardner MM, Norton RN, Buchner DM. Falls prevention over 2 years: A randomized controlled trial in women 80 years and older. Age Ageing 1999;28:513–8.

51. Ray WA, Griffin MR. Prescribed medications and the risk of falling. Top Geriatr Rehabil 1990;5:12–20.

52. Thapa PB, Gideon P, Fought RL, Ray WA. Psychotropic drugs and risk of recurrent falls in ambulatory nursing home residents. Am J Epidemiol 1995;142:202–11.

53. Bell AJ, Talbot-Stern JK, Hennessy A. Characteristics and outcomes of older patients presenting to the emergency department after a fall: a retrospective analysis. Med J Aust 2000;173:179–82.

54. Tinetti ME, Doucette JT, Claus EB. Contribution of predisposing and situational risk factors to serious fall injuries. J Am Geriatr Soc 1995;43:1207–13.

55. Tinetti ME, Doucette J, Claus E, Marottoli R. Risk factors for serious injury during falls by older persons in the community. J Am Geriatr Soc 1995;43:1214–21.

56. Ellis AA, Trent RB. Do the risks and consequences of hospitalized fall injuries among older adults in California vary by type of fall? J Gerontol A Biol Sci Med Sci 2001;56:M686–M692.

57. Herndon JG, Helmick CG, Sattin RW, Stevens JA, DeVito C, Wingo PA. Chronic medical conditions and risk of fall injury events at home in older adults. J Am Geriatr Soc 1997;45:739–43.

58. Goodacre S, Than M, Goyder E, Joseph AP. Can the distance fallen predict serious injury after a fall from a height? J Trauma 1999;46:105–58.

59. Speechley M, Tinetti M. Falls and injuries in frail and vigorous community elderly persons. J Am Geriatr Soc 1991;39:46–52.

60. Meyer J. Age: 2000. Census 2000 brief. Washington, DC: US Census Bureau; 2001. No. C2KBR/01-12. Available at http://www.census.gov/prod/2001pubs/c2kbr01-12.pdf. Accessed May 17, 2010.

61. U.S. Census Bureau. Current population reports. Projections of the population of the United States by age, sex, race, and Hispanic origin: 1995–2050 (no. P-25-1130). Washington DC: US Census Bureau; 1996.

62. CDC. Web-based Injury Statistics Query and Reporting System. 10 leading causes of injury. Atlanta, GA: CDC. Available at: http://www.cdc.gov/injury/wisqars/nonfatal.html. Accessed February 23, 2010.

63. CDC. Web-based Injury Statistics Query and Reporting System. Injury mortality reports, 1997–2007. Atlanta, GA; CDC. Available at http://www.cdc.gov/injury/wisqars/fatal.html. Accessed February 23, 2010.

64. Beaman V, Annest JL, Mercy JA, et al. Lethality of firearm-related injuries in the United States population. Ann Emerg Med 2000;35:258–66.

65. Hardy MS. Behavior-oriented approaches to reducing youth gun violence. Future Child 2002;12:100–17.

66. Grossman DC, Cummings P, Koepsell TD et al. Firearm safety counseling in primary care pediatrics: a randomized control trial. Pediatrics 2000;10:22–6.

67. Teret SP, Culross PL. Product-oriented approaches to reducing youth gun violence. Future Child 2002;12:118–31.

68. Loftin C, McDowall D, Wiersema B, Cottey TJ. Effects of restrictive licensing of handguns on homicide and suicide in the District of Columbia. N Engl J Med 1991;325:1615–20.

69. Lampert MT, Silva PS. An update on the impact of gun control legislation on suicide. Psychiatr Q 1998;69:127–34.

70. Cummings P, Grossman DC, Rivara FP, Koepsell TD. State gun safe storage laws and child mortality due to firearms. JAMA 1997;278:1084–6.

71. Hahn RA, Bilukha O, Crosby A, et al. Firearms laws and the reduction of violence: a systematic review. Am J Prev Med 2005;28(2S1):40–71

72. Mihalic S, Irwin K, Elliot D, Fagan A, Hansen D. Blueprints for violence prevention. Washington, DC: US Department of Justice, Office of Justice Programs, Office of Juvenile Justice and Delinquency Prevention; 2001.

73. National Institute of Mental Health. Older adults: depression and suicide facts [fact sheet]. Bethesda, MD: National Institute of Mental Health. Available at http://www.nimh.nih.gov/health/publications/older-adults-depression-and-suicide-facts-fact-sheet/index.shtml. Accessed April 26, 2010.

74. Rockett RH, Wang S, Lian Y, et al. Suicide-associated comorbidity among U.S. males and females: a multiple cause of death analysis. Injury Prev 2007;13:311–5.

75. Purselle DC, Heninger M, Hanzlick R, et al. Differential association of socioeconomic status in ethnic and age-defined suicides. Psychiatry Res 2009;167:258–65.

76. Schmutte T, O'Connell M, Weiland M, et al. Stemming the tide of suicide in older white men: a call to action. Am J Mens Health 2009;3:189–200.

77. US Department of Transportation; National Highway Traffic Safety Administration. Fatality Analysis Reporting System General Estimates System: 2006 data summary. Washington, DC: National Highway Traffic Safety Administration; 2008. Available at http://www-nrd.nhtsa.dot.gov/Pubs/2006%20DATA%20SUMMARY.PDF. Accessed April 2, 2010.

78. US Department of Transportation; Federal Highway Administration. Highway statistics, 2008. Washington, DC: Federal Highway Administration; 2010. Available at http://www.fhwa.dot.gov/policy-information/statistics/2008/dl20.cfm. Accessed March 8, 2011.

79. US Dept of Transportation; National Highway Traffic Safety Administration. Traffic safety facts. Seat belt use in 2010—overall results. Washington, DC: National Highway Traffic Safety Administration; 2010. Report no. DOR HS 811 378. Available at http://www-nrd.nhtsa.dot.gov/Pubs/811378.pdf. Accessed March 30, 2011.

80. Beck LF, Shults RA. Seat belt use in states and territories with primary and secondary laws—United States, 2006. J Safety Res 2009;40:469–72.

81. Beck LF, Shults RA, Mack KA, Ryan GW. Associations between socio-demographics and safety belt use in states with and without primary enforcement laws. Am J Public Health 2007;97:1619–24.

82. Boyd R, Kresnow MJ, Dellinger AM. Adult seat belt use: does the presence of children in the household make a difference? Traffic Inj Prev 2008;9:414–20.

83. US Department of Transportation; National Highway Traffic Safety Administration. Traffic safety facts. 2006 data. Children. Washington, DC: National Highway Traffic Safety Administration. Report no. DOT HS 810 803. Available at http://www-nrd.nhtsa.dot.gov/Pubs/810803.PDF. Accessed April 2, 2010.

84. Boyd R, Kresnow MJ, Dellinger AM. Alcohol-impaired driving and children in the household. Comm Health 2009;32:167–74.

85. Margolis LH, Foss RD, Tolbert WG. Alcohol and motor vehicle-related deaths of children as passengers, pedestrians, and bicyclists. JAMA 2000;283:2245–48.

86. US Dept of Transportation; National Highway Traffic Safety Administration. Traffic safety facts: 2006 data, Alcohol-impaired driving. Washington, DC: National Highway Traffic Safety Administration; 2008. Report no. DOT HS 810 801. Available at http://www-nrd.nhtsa.dot.gov/Pubs/810801.PDF. Accessed April 2, 2010.

87. Quinlan KP, Brewer RD, Sleet DA, Dellinger AM. Characteristics of child passenger deaths and injuries involving drinking drivers. JAMA 2000;283:2249–52.

88. CDC. CDC health disparities and inequalities report—United States, 2011. MMWR 2011;60(Suppl)52–5.

89. Rutland-Brown W, Wallace D, Faul M, Langlois JA. Traumatic brain injury hospitalizations among American Indians/Alaska Natives. J Head Trauma Rehab 2005;20;205–14.

90. US Department of Transportation; National Highway Traffic Safety Administration. Traffic safety facts. 2007 data. Older population. Washington, DC: National Highway Traffic Safety Administration. Report no. DOT HS 810 992. Available at http://www-nrd.nhtsa.dot.gov/Pubs/810992.PDF. Accessed April 2, 2010.

91. Naumann RB, Dellinger AM, Anderson ML, Bonomi AE, Rivara FP, Thompson RS. Preferred modes of travel among older adults: what factors affect the choice to walk instead of drive? J Safety Res 2009;40:395–8.

92. Beck LF, Dellinger AM, O'Neil ME. Motor vehicle crash injury rates by mode of travel, United States: using exposure-based methods to quantify differences. Am J Epidemiol 2007;166;212–8.

93. US Department of Transportation; National Highway Traffic Safety Administration. Traffic safety facts 2008. Report no. DOT HS-811-159. Washington, DC: National Highway Traffic Safety Administration; 2009. Available at http://www-nrd.nhtsa.dot.gov/pubs/811170.pdf. Accessed March 8, 2011.

94. US Department of Transportation; National Highway Traffic Safety Administration. Traffic safety facts. Laws. Motorcycle helmet use laws. Washington, DC: National Highway Traffic Safety Administration; 2008. Report no. DOT HS 810 887W. Available at http://www.dor.state.ne.us/nohs/pdf/TSFMCHelmetUseLaws2008.pdf. Accessed March 8, 2011.

95. Goldstein JP. The effect of motorcycle helmet use on the probability of fatality and the severity of head and neck injuries: a latent variable framework. Evaluation Rev 1986;10:355–75.

96. Sarkar S, Peek C, Kraus JF. Fatal injuries in motorcycle riders according to helmet use. J Trauma 1995;38:242–5.

97. Orsay EM, Muelleman RL, Peterson TD, Jurisic DH, Kosasih JB, Levy P. Motorcycle helmets and spinal injuries: dispelling the myth. Annals Emerg Med 1994;23:802–6.

98. Crompton JG, Bone C, Oyetunji T, Pollack KM, et al. Motorcycle helmets associated with lower risk of cervical spine injury: debunking the myth. J Am Coll Surg 2011;212:295–300.

99. Kraus J F, Peek C, Williams A. Compliance with the 1992 California motorcycle helmet use law. Am J Public Health 1995;85:96–9.

100. Kraus JF, Peek C, McArthur DL, Williams AF. The effect of the 1992 California motorcycle helmet usage law on motorcycle crash fatalities and injuries. JAMA 1994;272:1506–11.

101. Peek-Asa C, Kraus JF. Estimates of injury impairment after acute traumatic brain injury in motorcycle crashes before and after passage of a mandatory helmet use law. Ann Emerg Med 1997;29:630–6.

102. Ulmer RG, Northrup VS Evaluation of the repeal of the all-rider motorcycle helmet law in Florida. Report no. DOT HS-809-849. Washington, DC: National Highway Traffic Safety Administration; 2005.

103. Kyrychenko SY, McCartt AT. Florida weakened motorcycle helmet law: effects on death rates in motorcycle crashes. Traffic Inj Prev 2006;7:55–60.

104. US Department of Transportation. National Highway Traffic Safety Administration. Without motorcycle helmets, we all pay the price. Washington, DC: National Highway Traffic Safety Administration; 2005. Available at http://www.nhtsa.gov/people/injury/pedbimot/motorcycle/safebike/index.html. Accessed March 8, 2011.

105. US General Accounting Office. Highway safety: motorcycle helmet laws save lives and reduce costs to society. Washington, DC: US General Accounting Office; 1991. Available at http://www.gao.gov/products/RCED-91-170. Accessed March 8, 2011.

106. Insurance Institute for Highway Safety. Current US motorcycle and bicycle helmet laws. Arlington, VA: Insurance Institute for Highway Safety. Available at http://www.iihs.org/laws/helmetusecurrent.aspx. Accessed July 01, 2010.

107. CDC. Fatalities and injuries from falls among older adults—United States, 1993–2003 and 2001–2005. MMWR 2006;55:1221–4.

108. Coronado V, Thomas K, Sattin R, Johnson RL. 2005. The CDC traumatic brain injury surveillance system: Characteristics of persons aged 65 years and older hospitalized with a TBI. J Head Trauma Rehabil 2005;20:215–28.

109. Stevens JA, Corso PS, Finkelstein EA, Miller TR. The costs of fatal and nonfatal falls among older adults. Injury Prevention. 2006;12:290–5.

110. CDC. Self-reported falls and fall-related injuries among persons aged >65 years—United States, 2006. MMWR 2008;57;225–9.

111. Stevens JA, Sogolow ED. Gender differences for non-fatal unintentional fall related injuries among older adults. Inj Prev 2005;11:115–9.

112. National Alliance for Caregiving and AARP. Caregiving in the U.S. National Alliance for Caregiving and AARP; 2004 Available from http://www.caregiving.org/data/04finalreport.pdf. Accessed July 15, 2010.

113. McGuire LC, Ford ES, Ajani UA. Cognitive functioning as a predictor of functional disability in later life. Am J Geriatr Psychiatry 2006;14:36–42.

114. Talley RC, Crews JE. Framing the public health of caregiving. Am J Public Health 2007;97:224–8.

115. US Census Bureau. National population projections [database]. Table 094. Midyear population, by age and sex. Washington, DC: US Census Bureau. Available at http://www.census.gov/population/www/projections/natdet-D1A.html. Accessed March 8, 2011.

116. US Census Bureau. State and national population projections. Washington, DC: US Census Bureau. Available at http://www.census.gov/population/www/projections/popproj.html. Accessed March 8, 2011.

117. Campbell P; US Census Bureau. Population projections for states by age, sex, race, and Hispanic origin: 1995 to 2025. No. PPL-47. Washington, DC: US Census Bureau. Available at http://www.census.gov/population/www/projections/ppl47.html.

118. CDC. Medical examiners' and coroners' handbook on death registration and fetal death reporting; 2003 revision. Hyattsville, MD: National Center for Health Statistics; 2003. Available at http://www.cdc.gov/nchs/data/misc/hb_me.pdf. Accessed March 8, 2011.

119. CDC. Model state vital statistics act and regulations: 1992 revision. Hyattsville, MD: National Center for Health Statistics; 1995. Available at http://www.cdc.gov/nchs/data/misc/mvsact92b.pdf. Accessed March 8, 2011.

120. CDC. Proceedings of the international collaborative effort on injury statistics: volume I. Hyattsville, MD: National Center for Health Statistics; 1995.

121. Moyer L, Boyle C, Pollock D. Validity of death certificates for injury-related causes of death. Am J Epidemiol 1989;130:1024–32.

122. Barber C, Hemenway D, Hochstadt J, Azrael D. Underestimates of unintentional firearm fatalities: comparing supplementary homicide report data with the National Vital Statistics System. Injury Prevention 2002;8:252–6.

123. Romano P, McLoughlin E. Unspecified injuries on death certificates: a source of bias in injury research. Am J Epidemiol 1992;136:863–72.

124. Arias E, Schauman WS, Eschbach K, Sorlie PD, et al. The validity of race and Hispanic origin reporting on death certificates in the United States. Vital Health Stat 2008;2(148):1–23.

125. CDC. Preventing falls among seniors. What YOU can do to prevent falls. Atlanta, GA: CDC. Available at http://www.cdc.gov/ncipc/duip/spotlite/falls.htm. Accessed April 29, 2010.

126. Hardy MS. Behavior-oriented approaches to reducing gun violence. The Future of Children: A Collaboration of The Woodrow Wilson School of Public and International Affairs at Princeton University and The Brookings Institution 2002;12:101–8.

127. CDC. First reports evaluating the effectiveness of strategies for preventing violence: firearms laws. Findings from the Task Force on Community Preventive Services. MMWR 2003;52(No. RR-14):11–20.

TABLE 1. ICD–9 and ICD–10 codes for external cause of traumatic brain injury

Description	ICD–9	ICD–10
Motor vehicle traffic–related (unintentional)	E810–E819	V02–V04 (.1, .9), V09.2, V12–V14 (.3–.9), V19 (.4–.6), V20–V28 (.3–.9), V29–V79 (.4–.9), V80 (.3–.5), V81.1, V82.1, V83–V86 (.0–.3), V87 (.0–.8), V89.2
Occupant	E810–E819 (.0, .1)	V30–V79 (.4–.9), V83–V86 (.0–.3)
Motorcycle	E810–E819 (.2, .3)	V20–V28 (.3–.9), V29 (.4–.9)
Pedal cycle	E810–E819 (.6)	V12–V14 (.3–.9), V19 (.4–.6)
Pedestrian	E810–E819 (.7)	V02–V04 (.1, .9), V09.2
Other/Unspecified	E810–E819 (.4, .5, .8, .9)	V80 (.3–.5), V81.1, V82.1, V87 (.0–.8), V89.2
Falls	E880–E886, E888, E957, E968.1, E987	W00–W19, X80, Y01, Y30
Firearms	E922, E955 (.0–.4), E965 (.0–.4), E970, E985 (.0–.4)	U01.4, W32–W34, X72–X74, X93–X95, Y22–Y24, Y35.0
Suicide	E955 (.0–.4)	X72–X74
Homicide	E965 (.0–.4)	U01.4, X93–X95
Other	E922, E970, E985 (.0–.4)	W32–W34, Y22–Y24, Y35.0
Other/Unspecified	All other E codes	All other cause codes

Abbreviations: ICD-9 = *International Classification of Diseases, Ninth Revision*; ICD-10 = *International Classification of Diseases, Tenth Revision*.

TABLE 2. Numbers and age-adjusted rates per 100,000 population for traumatic brain injury deaths, by year, sex, and race/ethnicity — United States, 1997–2007

Year	Sex	White, non-Hispanic			Black, non-Hispanic			American Indian/ Alaska Native			Hispanic			Other/ Unknown	Total		
		No.	Rate	(95% CI)	No.	Rate	(95% CI)	No.	Rate	(95% CI)	No.	Rate	(95% CI)	No.	No.	Rate	(95% CI)
1997	M	28,165	30.0	(29.7–30.4)	5,571	37.2	(36.1–38.2)	465	50.7	(45.4–56.1)	3,468	24.8	(23.8–25.8)	854	38,523	30.5	(30.2–30.8)
	F	10,887	9.9	(9.7–10.1)	1,707	10.0	(9.5–10.4)	153	15.4	(12.7–18.0)	836	6.3	(5.8–6.8)	357	13,940	9.6	(9.4–9.8)
	Total	39,052	19.3	(19.1–19.5)	7,278	22.4	(21.8–22.9)	618	32.0	(29.2–34.8)	4,304	15.3	(14.8–15.8)	1,211	52,463	19.3	(19.2–19.5)
1998	M	28,293	30.0	(29.6–30.4)	5,334	35.7	(34.7–36.8)	423	41.6	(37.1–46.1)	3,444	23.9	(22.9–24.9)	842	38,336	30.1	(29.8–30.4)
	F	11,143	10.0	(9.8–10.2)	1,598	9.2	(8.8–9.7)	179	16.6	(14.1–19.2)	887	6.7	(6.2–7.2)	363	14,170	9.6	(9.4–9.8)
	Total	39,436	19.3	(19.1–19.5)	6,932	21.2	(20.7–21.7)	602	28.5	(26.0–30.9)	4,331	15.1	(14.6–15.6)	1,205	52,506	19.1	(19.0–19.3)
1999	M	27,884	29.4	(29.0–29.7)	5,166	34.4	(33.4–35.4)	441	43.4	(38.9–48.0)	3,445	23.8	(22.8–24.8)	829	37,765	29.3	(29.0–29.6)
	F	11,145	9.8	(9.7–10.0)	1,638	9.4	(8.9–9.9)	165	15.7	(13.1–18.2)	870	6.3	(5.8–6.7)	358	14,176	9.4	(9.3–9.6)
	Total	39,029	18.9	(18.7–19.1)	6,804	20.7	(20.2–21.2)	606	29.0	(26.5–31.5)	4,315	14.7	(14.2–15.2)	1,187	51,941	18.7	(18.5–18.8)
2000	M	27,357	28.6	(28.2–28.9)	4,947	31.7	(30.8–32.7)	421	40.0	(35.7–44.3)	3,656	23.2	(22.3–24.2)	808	37,189	28.3	(28.0–28.6)
	F	10,528	9.4	(9.2–9.5)	1,502	8.4	(8.0–8.8)	170	14.7	(12.4–16.9)	939	6.6	(6.1–7.1)	352	13,491	8.9	(8.8–9.1)
	Total	37,885	18.3	(18.2–18.5)	6,449	19.0	(18.6–19.5)	591	26.6	(24.3–28.9)	4,595	14.8	(14.3–15.3)	1,160	50,680	18.0	(17.8–18.1)
2001	M	28,634	29.6	(29.3–30.0)	5,028	32.0	(31.0–32.9)	437	40.3	(36.1–44.5)	3,921	23.3	(22.4–24.2)	855	38,875	29.2	(28.9–29.5)
	F	10,883	9.5	(9.3–9.7)	1,457	8.2	(7.7–8.6)	190	16.7	(14.2–19.2)	989	6.7	(6.2–7.2)	366	13,885	9.0	(8.9–9.2)
	Total	39,517	18.9	(18.7–19.1)	6,485	19.0	(18.5–19.5)	627	28.0	(25.6–30.3)	4,910	14.9	(14.5–15.4)	1,221	52,760	18.5	(18.3–18.6)
2002	M	28,519	29.2	(28.9–)29.5)	4,909	30.9	(30.0–31.8)	485	42.8	(38.7–47.0)	3,968	23.0	(22.1–23.8)	890	38,771	28.7	(28.4–29.0)
	F	10,897	9.5	(9.3–9.7)	1,467	8.0	(7.6–8.5)	174	14.9	(12.6–17.2)	989	6.2	(5.8–6.6)	386	13,913	9.0	(8.8–9.1)
	Total	39,416	18.7	(18.6–18.9)	6,376	18.4	(17.9–18.9)	659	28.4	(26.1–30.7)	4,957	14.4	(14.0–14.9)	1,276	52,684	18.2	(18.1–18.4)
2003	M	28,394	28.9	(28.5–29.2)	5,030	31.0	(30.0–31.9)	503	45.3	(40.9–49.6)	4,023	22.4	(21.5–23.2)	825	38,775	28.4	(28.1–28.7)
	F	10,937	9.4	(9.2–9.5)	1,539	8.4	(8.0–8.9)	166	14.7	(12.3–17.0)	1,068	6.7	(6.2–7.1)	398	14,108	8.9	(8.8–9.1)
	Total	39,331	18.5	(18.3–18.7)	6,569	18.8	(18.3–19.2)	669	29.4	(27.0–31.8)	5,091	14.5	(14.0–14.9)	1,223	52,883	18.1	(17.9–18.2)
2004	M	28,502	28.7	(28.4–29.0)	4,934	30.6	(29.7–31.5)	439	38.5	(34.5–42.4)	3,996	21.3	(20.6–22.1)	755	38,626	27.9	(27.6–28.2)
	F	11,391	9.7	(9.5–9.9)	1,510	8.2	(7.7–8.6)	166	13.4	(11.3–15.5)	1,040	6.3	(5.8–6.7)	417	14,524	9.1	(8.9–9.2)
	Total	39,893	18.6	(18.4–18.8)	6,444	18.3	(17.9–18.8)	605	25.3	(23.2–27.4)	5,036	13.8	(13.4–14.2)	1,172	53,150	18.0	(17.8–18.1)
2005	M	29,497	29.4	(29.1–29.8)	5,229	31.5	(30.5–32.4)	478	39.6	(35.9–43.4)	4,324	22.7	(21.9–23.5)	884	40,412	28.8	(28.5–29.1)
	F	11,340	9.5	(9.3–9.7)	1,514	8.2	(7.8–8.6)	160	13.2	(11.1–15.3)	1,091	6.2	(5.8–6.6)	389	14,494	8.9	(8.8–9.1)
	Total	40,837	18.9	(18.7–19.1)	6,743	18.9	(18.4–19.3)	638	26.0	(23.9–28.1)	5,415	14.4	(14.0–14.9)	1,273	54,906	18.3	(18.2–18.5)
2006	M	29,119	28.7	(28.4–29.1)	5,296	31.2	(30.3–32.1)	460	38.5	(34.8–42.2)	4,322	21.7	(20.9–22.4)	832	40,029	28.1	(27.8–28.4)
	F	11,385	9.4	(9.3–9.6)	1,446	7.6	(7.2–8.0)	154	12.3	(10.3–14.3)	1,057	5.9	(5.5–6.2)	394	14,436	8.8	(8.6–8.9)
	Total	40,504	18.6	(18.4–18.7)	6,742	18.4	(18.0–18.9)	614	24.9	(22.9–27.0)	5,379	13.7	(13.3–14.2)	1,226	54,465	17.9	(17.8–18.1)
2007	M	29,593	28.9	(28.6–29.3)	5,069	29.0	(28.1–29.8)	429	36.3	(32.6–40.0)	4,197	20.8	(20.1–21.5)	884	40,172	27.9	(27.6–28.2)
	F	11,462	9.3	(9.2–9.5)	1,441	7.5	(7.1–7.9)	145	11.7	(9.8–13.7)	1,086	5.8	(5.5–6.2)	410	14,544	8.7	(8.5–8.8)
	Total	41,055	18.6	(18.4–18.8)	6,510	17.5	(17.1–17.9)	574	23.6	(21.6–25.6)	5,283	13.3	(12.9–13.7)	1,294	54,716	17.8	(17.6–17.9)
Total	M	313,957	29.2	(29.1–29.4)	56,513	32.2	(31.9–32.5)	4,981	41.3	(40.0–42.5)	42,764	22.7	(22.4–22.9)	9,258	427,473	28.8	(28.7–28.9)
	F	121,998	9.6	(9.5–9.7)	16,819	8.4	(8.3–8.6)	1,822	14.4	(13.7–15.1)	10,852	6.3	(6.2–6.4)	4,190	155,681	9.1	(9.0–9.1)
	Total	435,955	18.8	(18.8–18.9)	73,332	19.3	(19.1–19.4)	6,803	27.3	(26.6–27.9)	53,616	14.4	(14.2–14.5)	13,448	583,154	18.4	(18.3–18.4)

Abbreviations: CI = confidence interval; F = female; M = male.

TABLE 3. Numbers and rates per 100,000 population for traumatic brain injury deaths, by year, sex, and age group — United States, 1997–2007

		Age group (yrs)												
		0–4			5–9			10–14			15–19			
Year	Sex	No.	Rate	(95% CI)	No.	Rate	(95% CI)	No.	Rate	(95% CI)	No.	Rate	(95% CI)
1997	M	635	6.5	(5.9–7.0)	378	3.6	(3.3–4.0)	669	6.7	(6.2–7.2)	3,743	37.5	(36.3–38.7)
	F	512	5.5	(5.0–5.9)	262	2.7	(2.3–3.0)	358	3.7	(3.4–4.1)	1,253	13.3	(12.6–14.0)
	Total	1,147	6.0	(5.6–6.3)	640	3.2	(2.9–3.4)	1,027	5.2	(4.9–5.6)	4,996	25.8	(25.0–26.5)
1998	M	664	6.8	(6.3–7.3)	407	3.9	(3.5–4.3)	722	7.1	(6.6–7.6)	3,551	34.8	(33.7–36.0)
	F	490	5.2	(4.8–5.7)	257	2.6	(2.3–2.9)	338	3.5	(3.1–3.9)	1,251	13.0	(12.3–13.7)
	Total	1,154	6.0	(5.7–6.4)	664	3.2	(3.0–3.5)	1,060	5.3	(5.0–5.7)	4,802	24.2	(23.5–24.9)
1999	M	610	6.2	(5.7–6.7)	379	3.6	(3.2–4.0)	577	5.6	(5.1–6.0)	3,414	33.1	(32.0–34.2)
	F	435	4.7	(4.2–5.1)	254	2.5	(2.2–2.8)	304	3.1	(2.7–3.4)	1,213	12.4	(11.7–13.1)
	Total	1,045	5.5	(5.1–5.8)	633	3.1	(2.8–3.3)	881	4.4	(4.1–4.6)	4,627	23.0	(22.4–23.7)
2000	M	628	6.4	(5.9–6.9)	358	3.4	(3.1–3.8)	551	5.2	(4.8–5.7)	3,377	32.4	(31.3–33.5)
	F	449	4.8	(4.3–5.2)	266	2.7	(2.3–3.0)	278	2.8	(2.4–3.1)	1,162	11.8	(11.1–12.5)
	Total	1,077	5.6	(5.3–5.9)	624	3.0	(2.8–3.3)	829	4.0	(3.7–4.3)	4,539	22.4	(21.7–23.0)
2001	M	619	6.2	(5.7–6.7)	329	3.2	(2.8–3.5)	534	5.0	(4.6–5.4)	3,204	30.5	(29.5–31.6)
	F	440	4.6	(4.2–5.1)	239	2.4	(2.1–2.7)	263	2.6	(2.3–2.9)	1,061	10.7	(10.1–11.4)
	Total	1,059	5.5	(5.1–5.8)	568	2.8	(2.6–3.0)	797	3.8	(3.5–4.1)	4,265	20.9	(20.3–21.6)
2002	M	569	5.7	(5.2–6.1)	286	2.8	(2.5–3.1)	502	4.6	(4.2–5.0)	3,246	30.8	(29.7–31.9)
	F	417	4.3	(3.9–4.8)	217	2.2	(1.9–2.5)	283	2.7	(2.4–3.1)	1,099	11.1	(10.4–11.7)
	Total	986	5.0	(4.7–5.3)	503	2.5	(2.3–2.7)	785	3.7	(3.5–4.0)	4,345	21.2	(20.6–21.9)
2003	M	621	6.1	(5.6–6.6)	276	2.7	(2.4–3.0)	558	5.1	(4.7–5.6)	3,028	28.6	(27.6–29.6)
	F	444	4.6	(4.1–5.0)	179	1.9	(1.6–2.1)	260	2.5	(2.2–2.8)	1,034	10.3	(9.7–11.0)
	Total	1,065	5.3	(5.0–5.7)	455	2.3	(2.1–2.5)	818	3.9	(3.6–4.1)	4,062	19.7	(19.1–20.4)
2004	M	569	5.5	(5.0–6.0)	257	2.6	(2.2–2.9)	492	4.5	(4.1–5.0)	2,929	27.4	(26.4–28.4)
	F	447	4.5	(4.1–4.9)	190	2.0	(1.7–2.3)	269	2.6	(2.3–2.9)	1,073	10.6	(10.0–11.2)
	Total	1,016	5.0	(4.7–5.3)	447	2.3	(2.1–2.5)	761	3.6	(3.3–3.9)	4,002	19.2	(18.6–19.8)
2005	M	602	5.8	(5.3–6.2)	235	2.3	(2.0–2.6)	455	4.3	(3.9–4.7)	2,970	27.4	(26.4–28.4)
	F	452	4.5	(4.1–4.9)	205	2.1	(1.8–2.4)	230	2.3	(2.0–2.6)	994	9.7	(9.1–10.3)
	Total	1,054	5.1	(4.8–5.5)	440	2.2	(2.0–2.5)	685	3.3	(3.0–3.5)	3,964	18.8	(18.2–19.4)
2006	M	589	5.6	(5.1–6.0)	261	2.6	(2.3–2.9)	410	3.9	(3.5–4.3)	2,905	26.5	(25.5–27.4)
	F	413	4.1	(3.7–4.5)	177	1.8	(1.6–2.1)	227	2.3	(2.0–2.6)	972	9.3	(8.8–9.9)
	Total	1,002	4.9	(4.6–5.2)	438	2.2	(2.0–2.4)	637	3.1	(2.9–3.3)	3,877	18.1	(17.6–18.7)
2007	M	555	5.2	(4.8–5.6)	220	2.1	(1.9–2.4)	384	3.7	(3.3–4.1)	2,643	23.9	(23.0–24.8)
	F	423	4.1	(3.7–4.5)	162	1.7	(1.4–1.9)	209	2.1	(1.8–2.4)	904	8.6	(8.1–9.2)
	Total	978	4.7	(4.4–5.0)	382	1.9	(1.7–2.1)	593	2.9	(2.7–3.2)	3,547	16.4	(15.9–17.0)
Total	M	6,661	6.0	(5.8–6.1)	3,386	3.0	(2.9–3.1)	5,854	5.0	(4.9–5.2)	35,010	30.2	(29.8–30.5)
	F	4,922	4.6	(4.5–4.7)	2,408	2.2	(2.1–2.3)	3,019	2.7	(2.6–2.8)	12,016	10.9	(10.8–11.1)
	Total	11,583	5.3	(5.2–5.4)	5,794	2.6	(2.6–2.7)	8,873	3.9	(3.8–4.0)	47,026	20.8	(20.6–21.0)

Abbreviations: CI = confidence interval; F = female; M = male.

TABLE 3. *(Continued)* Numbers and rates per 100,000 population for traumatic brain injury deaths, by year, sex, and age group — United States, 1997–2007

		Age group (yrs)											
		20–24			25–34			35–44			45–54		
Year	Sex	No.	Rate	(95% CI)	No.	Rate	(95% CI)	No.	Rate	(95% CI)	No.	Rate	(95% CI)
1997	M	4,197	46.0	(44.6–47.4)	6,528	31.4	(30.7–32.2)	6,031	27.5	(26.8–28.2)	4,449	26.6	(25.8–27.3)
	F	941	10.7	(10.0–11.4)	1,720	8.4	(8.0–8.8)	1,857	8.3	(8.0–8.7)	1,289	7.4	(7.0–7.8)
	Total	5,138	28.7	(27.9–29.5)	8,248	19.9	(19.5–20.4)	7,888	17.8	(17.4–18.2)	5,738	16.8	(16.4–17.2)
1998	M	4,099	44.2	(42.9–45.6)	6,012	29.3	(28.6–30.1)	5,972	26.9	(26.2–27.5)	4,537	26.3	(25.5–27.0)
	F	863	9.7	(9.0–10.3)	1,656	8.2	(7.8–8.6)	1,884	8.4	(8.0–8.7)	1,338	7.5	(7.1–7.8)
	Total	4,962	27.3	(26.6–28.1)	7,668	18.8	(18.4–19.2)	7,856	17.6	(17.2–17.9)	5,875	16.7	(16.2–17.1)
1999	M	3,999	42.1	(40.8–43.4)	5,749	28.4	(27.7–29.1)	5,873	26.2	(25.5–26.9)	4,613	25.7	(25.0–26.4)
	F	881	9.7	(9.0–10.3)	1,515	7.6	(7.2–8.0)	1,816	8.0	(7.6–8.4)	1,334	7.2	(6.8–7.5)
	Total	4,880	26.2	(25.5–27.0)	7,264	18.1	(17.7–18.5)	7,689	17.1	(16.7–17.4)	5,947	16.3	(15.8–16.7)
2000	M	4,011	41.0	(39.8–42.3)	5,595	27.8	(27.1–28.6)	5,949	26.5	(25.8–27.2)	4,957	26.6	(25.8–27.3)
	F	930	9.9	(9.3–10.6)	1,464	7.4	(7.0–7.8)	1,717	7.6	(7.2–7.9)	1,339	6.9	(6.6–7.3)
	Total	4,941	25.8	(25.1–26.6)	7,059	17.7	(17.3–18.1)	7,666	17.0	(16.6–17.4)	6,296	16.6	(16.2–17.0)
2001	M	4,258	42.1	(40.8–43.3)	5,815	29.1	(28.3–29.8)	6,079	27.1	(26.4–27.8)	5,339	27.6	(26.9–28.4)
	F	886	9.2	(8.6–9.8)	1,371	7.0	(6.6–7.4)	1,745	7.7	(7.3–8.1)	1,478	7.4	(7.0–7.8)
	Total	5,144	26.0	(25.3–26.7)	7,186	18.2	(17.7–18.6)	7,824	17.4	(17.0–17.7)	6,817	17.3	(16.9–17.7)
2002	M	4,214	40.5	(39.3–41.7)	5,768	28.8	(28.1–29.6)	5,776	26.0	(25.3–26.6)	5,408	27.6	(26.9–28.3)
	F	963	9.7	(9.1–10.3)	1,345	6.9	(6.5–7.3)	1,740	7.8	(7.4–8.1)	1,499	7.4	(7.0–7.8)
	Total	5,177	25.5	(24.8–26.2)	7,113	18.0	(17.6–18.4)	7,516	16.8	(16.4–17.2)	6,907	17.3	(16.9–17.7)
2003	M	4,158	39.3	(38.1–40.5)	5,584	27.9	(27.2–28.7)	5,745	26.1	(25.4–26.8)	5,550	27.8	(27.0–28.5)
	F	966	9.6	(9.0–10.2)	1,304	6.7	(6.3–7.0)	1,630	7.4	(7.0–7.7)	1,573	7.6	(7.2–8.0)
	Total	5,124	24.8	(24.1–25.4)	6,888	17.4	(17.0–17.8)	7,375	16.7	(16.3–17.1)	7,123	17.5	(17.1–17.9)
2004	M	4,166	38.7	(37.5–39.9)	5,456	27.2	(26.4–27.9)	5,404	24.7	(24.0–25.4)	5,734	28.1	(27.4–28.9)
	F	938	9.2	(8.6–9.8)	1,365	7.0	(6.6–7.4)	1,597	7.3	(6.9–7.6)	1,628	7.7	(7.3–8.1)
	Total	5,104	24.4	(23.7–25.0)	6,821	17.2	(16.8–17.6)	7,001	16.0	(15.6–16.3)	7,362	17.7	(17.3–18.1)
2005	M	4,239	39.0	(37.9–40.2)	5,812	28.9	(28.1–29.6)	5,565	25.6	(24.9–26.3)	6,043	29.0	(28.3–29.8)
	F	865	8.5	(7.9–9.0)	1,311	6.7	(6.3–7.1)	1,571	7.2	(6.9–7.6)	1,570	7.3	(6.9–7.7)
	Total	5,104	24.2	(23.5–24.9)	7,123	17.9	(17.5–18.4)	7,136	16.4	(16.0–16.8)	7,613	18.0	(17.6–18.4)
2006	M	4,217	38.6	(37.4–39.8)	5,622	27.7	(27.0–28.4)	5,358	24.7	(24.1–25.4)	6,113	28.8	(28.1–29.6)
	F	896	8.8	(8.2–9.3)	1,201	6.1	(5.8–6.5)	1,547	7.2	(6.8–7.5)	1,675	7.6	(7.3–8.0)
	Total	5,113	24.2	(23.5–24.8)	6,823	17.1	(16.7–17.5)	6,905	16.0	(15.6–16.3)	7,788	18.1	(17.7–18.5)
2007	M	4,151	37.9	(36.8–39.1)	5,611	27.3	(26.6–28.0)	5,184	24.2	(23.5–24.8)	6,167	28.6	(27.9–29.4)
	F	853	8.3	(7.8–8.9)	1,251	6.3	(6.0–6.7)	1,467	6.9	6.5–7.2	1,608	7.2	(6.9–7.6)
	Total	5,004	23.6	(22.9–24.2)	6,862	17.0	(16.6–17.4)	6,651	15.5	15.1–15.9	7,775	17.8	(17.4–18.2)
Total	M	45,709	40.7	(40.3–41.1)	63,552	28.5	(28.3–28.8)	62,936	26.0	25.7–26.2	58,910	27.6	(27.4–27.8)
	F	9,982	9.4	(9.2–9.5)	15,503	7.1	(7.0–7.2)	18,571	7.6	7.5–7.7	16,331	7.4	(7.3–7.5)
	Total	55,691	25.4	(25.2–25.6)	79,055	18.0	(17.8–18.1)	81,507	16.7	16.6–16.9	75,241	17.3	(17.2–17.4)

Abbreviations: CI = confidence interval; F = female; M = male.

TABLE 3. *(Continued)* Numbers and rates per 100,000 population for traumatic brain injury deaths, by year, sex, and age group — United States, 1997–2007

		Age group (yrs)												
		55–64			65–74			75–84			≥85			
Year	Sex	No.	Rate	(95% CI)	No.	Rate	(95% CI)	No.	Rate	(95% CI)	No.	Rate	(95% CI)
1997	M	3,174	30.0	(29.0–31.1)	3,354	40.1	(38.8–41.5)	3,594	78.0	(75.5–80.6)	1,739	158.1	(150.6–165.5)
	F	901	7.8	(7.3–8.3)	1,235	12.0	(11.3–12.6)	1,888	26.2	(25.0–27.4)	1,715	61.1	(58.2–64.0)
	Total	4,075	18.4	(17.9–19.0)	4,589	24.6	(23.9–25.3)	5,482	46.4	(45.2–47.6)	3,454	88.4	(85.5–91.4)
1998	M	3,247	29.5	(28.4–30.5)	3,300	39.6	(38.2–41.0)	3,849	81.7	(79.1–84.3)	1,929	168.2	(160.7–175.7)
	F	935	7.8	(7.3–8.3)	1,253	12.2	(11.6–12.9)	2,053	28.1	(26.9–29.3)	1,845	63.9	(61.0–66.9)
	Total	4,182	18.2	(17.6–18.7)	4,553	24.5	(23.8–25.2)	5,902	49.1	(47.9–50.4)	3,774	93.6	(90.6–96.6)
1999	M	3,224	28.3	(27.3–29.3)	3,358	40.5	(39.1–41.9)	3,887	80.7	(78.2–83.3)	2,050	171.8	(164.4–179.2)
	F	973	7.9	(7.4–8.4)	1,282	12.7	(12.0–13.4)	2,067	27.9	(26.7–29.1)	2,096	70.8	(67.8–73.8)
	Total	4,197	17.7	(17.1–18.2)	4,640	25.2	(24.5–25.9)	5,954	48.7	(47.5–49.9)	4,146	99.8	(96.8–102.8)
2000	M	3,205	27.4	(26.4–28.3)	3,021	36.4	(35.1–37.7)	3,615	73.6	(71.2–76.0)	1,898	153.3	(146.4–160.2)
	F	992	7.8	(7.3–8.3)	1,172	11.6	(11.0–12.3)	1,905	25.3	(24.2–26.5)	1,813	59.8	(57.0–62.5)
	Total	4,197	17.2	(16.7–17.7)	4,193	22.8	(22.1–23.5)	5,520	44.4	(43.2–45.6)	3,711	86.9	(84.1–89.7)
2001	M	3,383	28.1	(27.2–29.1)	3,264	39.3	(37.9–40.6)	3,958	78.9	(76.5–81.4)	2,059	162.0	(155.0–168.9)
	F	1,043	8.0	(7.5–8.5)	1,229	12.3	(11.6–12.9)	2,191	28.8	(27.6–30.0)	1,934	62.7	(59.9–65.5)
	Total	4,426	17.7	(17.2–18.2)	4,493	24.5	(23.8–25.2)	6,149	48.7	(47.5–49.9)	3,993	91.7	(88.9–94.5)
2002	M	3,691	28.9	(28.0–29.8)	3,305	39.7	(38.4–41.1)	3,927	76.7	(74.3–79.1)	2,046	156.4	(149.6–163.1)
	F	1,082	7.8	(7.4–8.3)	1,134	11.4	(10.7–12.0)	2,142	27.8	(26.6–29.0)	1,986	63.3	(60.6–66.1)
	Total	4,773	18.0	(17.5–18.5)	4,439	24.2	(23.5–25.0)	6,069	47.4	(46.2–48.5)	4,032	90.7	(87.9–93.5)
2003	M	3,886	29.0	(28.1–30.0)	3,162	37.7	(36.4–39.1)	4,004	76.9	(74.5–79.3)	2,185	160.5	(153.8–167.2)
	F	1,112	7.7	(7.3–8.2)	1,199	12.0	(11.3–12.7)	2,250	29.0	(27.8–30.2)	2,154	67.0	(64.2–69.9)
	Total	4,998	18.0	(17.5–18.5)	4,361	23.7	(23.0–24.4)	6,254	48.2	(47.0–49.4)	4,339	94.9	(92.0–97.7)
2004	M	4,021	28.8	(27.9–29.7)	3,291	38.9	(37.6–40.3)	4,008	75.9	(73.6–78.3)	2,270	161.3	(154.6–167.9)
	F	1,158	7.7	(7.2–8.1)	1,220	12.1	(11.5–12.8)	2,342	30.0	(28.8–31.2)	2,294	70.0	(67.1–72.9)
	Total	5,179	17.8	(17.4–18.3)	4,511	24.4	(23.7–25.1)	6,350	48.6	(47.4–49.8)	4,564	97.4	(94.6–100.3)
2005	M	4,333	29.7	(28.8–30.6)	3,322	38.9	(37.5–40.2)	4,390	82.1	(79.6–84.5)	2,431	164.6	(158.1–171.1)
	F	1,208	7.7	(7.3–8.1)	1,264	12.5	(11.8–13.2)	2,406	30.7	(29.5–32.0)	2,415	71.3	(68.5–74.2)
	Total	5,541	18.3	(17.8–18.8)	4,586	24.6	(23.9–25.3)	6,796	51.6	(50.4–52.8)	4,846	99.7	(96.9–102.5)
2006	M	4,440	29.2	(28.4–30.1)	3,369	38.8	(37.5–40.1)	4,266	79.2	(76.8–81.5)	2,460	158.1	(151.8–164.3)
	F	1,275	7.8	(7.4–8.2)	1,189	11.6	(10.9–12.3)	2,458	31.4	(30.2–32.7)	2,404	68.5	(65.8–71.3)
	Total	5,715	18.1	(17.7–18.6)	4,558	24.1	(23.4–24.8)	6,724	50.9	(49.7–52.1)	4,864	96.1	(93.4–98.8)
2007	M	4,653	29.5	(28.7–30.4)	3,480	39.0	(37.8–40.3)	4,376	80.7	(78.3–83.1)	2,738	167.4	(161.1–173.6)
	F	1,264	7.5	(7.1–7.9)	1,263	12.1	(11.4–12.7)	2,412	31.0	(29.7–32.2)	2,727	75.2	(72.3–78.0)
	Total	5,917	18.1	(17.7–18.6)	4,743	24.5	(23.8–25.2)	6,788	51.4	(50.1–52.6)	5,465	103.8	(101.1–106.6)
Total	M	41,257	29.0	(28.7–29.3)	36,226	39.0	(38.6–39.4)	43,874	78.6	(77.9–79.3)	23,805	162.0	(159.9–164.0)
	F	11,943	7.8	(7.6–7.9)	13,440	12.0	(11.8–12.2)	24,114	28.8	(28.4–29.2)	23,383	67.0	(66.1–67.8)
	Total	53,200	18.0	(17.8–18.1)	49,666	24.3	(24.1–24.5)	67,988	48.7	(48.3–49.1)	47,188	95.1	(94.3–96.0)

Abbreviations: CI = confidence interval; F = female; M = male.

TABLE 4. Average annual numbers and rates per 100,000 population for traumatic brain injury deaths, by age group, sex, and external mechanism of injury — United States, 1997–2007

Age group (yrs)	Sex	Falls			Firearms			Motor vehicles			Other/Unknown		
		No.	Rate	(95% CI)	No.	Rate	(95% CI)	No.	Rate	(95% CI)	No.	Rate	(95% CI)
0–4	M	27	0.3	(0.2–0.4)	26	0.3	(0.2–0.4)	239	2.4	(2.1–2.7)	314	3.1	(2.8–3.4)
	F	12	0.1	(0.1–0.2)	18	0.2	(0.1–0.3)	191	2.0	(1.7–2.3)	227	2.3	(2.0–2.6)
	Total	39	0.2	(0.1–0.3)	43	0.2	(0.2–0.3)	430	2.2	(2.0–2.4)	541	2.7	(2.5–3.0)
5–9	M	8	0.1	(0.0–0.2)	28	0.3	(0.2–0.4)	204	2.0	(1.7–2.3)	68	0.7	(0.5–0.8)
	F	5	0.1	(0.0–0.1)	19	0.2	(0.1–0.3)	152	1.5	(1.3–1.8)	43	0.4	(0.3–0.6)
	Total	12	0.1	(0.0–0.1)	47	0.2	(0.2–0.3)	356	1.8	(1.6–2.0)	112	0.6	(0.5–0.7)
10–14	M	13	0.1	(0.1–0.2)	150	1.4	(1.2–1.7)	285	2.7	(2.4–3.0)	85	0.8	(0.6–1.0)
	F	4	0.0	(0.0–0.1)	41	0.4	(0.3–0.6)	188	1.9	(1.6–2.1)	42	0.4	(0.3–0.6)
	Total	17	0.1	(0.0–0.1)	191	0.9	(0.8–1.1)	472	2.3	(2.1–2.5)	127	0.6	(0.5–0.7)
15–19	M	57	0.5	(0.4–0.7)	1,257	11.9	(11.3–12.6)	1,619	15.3	(14.6–16.1)	250	2.4	(2.1–2.7)
	F	12	0.1	(0.1–0.2)	185	1.9	(1.6–2.1)	817	8.2	(7.6–8.8)	78	0.8	(0.6–1.0)
	Total	70	0.3	(0.3–0.4)	1,441	7.0	(6.7–7.4)	2,436	11.9	(11.4–12.3)	328	1.6	(1.4–1.8)
20–24	M	99	1.0	(0.8–1.2)	1,881	18.4	(17.6–19.3)	1,829	17.9	(17.1–18.7)	346	3.4	(3.0–3.7)
	F	15	0.2	(0.1–0.3)	249	2.6	(2.2–2.9)	556	5.7	(5.3–6.2)	87	0.9	(0.7–1.1)
	Total	115	0.6	(0.5–0.7)	2,129	10.7	(10.2–11.1)	2,385	12.0	(11.5–12.5)	434	2.2	(2.0–2.4)
25–34	M	201	1.0	(0.9–1.1)	2,797	13.8	(13.3–14.3)	2,124	10.5	(10.0–10.9)	655	3.2	(3.0–3.5)
	F	33	0.2	(0.1–0.2)	485	2.4	(2.2–2.7)	702	3.5	(3.3–3.8)	190	1.0	(0.8–1.1)
	Total	234	0.6	(0.5–0.7)	3,282	8.2	(7.9–8.5)	2,826	7.1	(6.8–7.3)	845	2.1	(2.0–2.3)
35–44	M	375	1.7	(1.5–1.9)	2,590	11.7	(11.3–12.2)	1,826	8.3	(7.9–8.7)	930	4.2	(3.9–4.5)
	F	87	0.4	(0.3–0.5)	590	2.7	(2.4–2.9)	722	3.3	(3.0–3.5)	289	1.3	(1.2–1.5)
	Total	462	1.0	(0.9–1.1)	3,181	7.2	(6.9–7.4)	2,548	5.8	(5.5–6.0)	1,220	2.8	(2.6–2.9)
45–54	M	559	2.9	(2.6–3.1)	2,386	12.3	(11.8–12.8)	1,440	7.4	(7.0–7.8)	971	5.0	(4.7–5.3)
	F	166	0.8	(0.7–1.0)	491	2.4	(2.2–2.7)	557	2.8	(2.5–3.0)	270	1.3	(1.2–1.5)
	Total	725	1.8	(1.7–2.0)	2,877	7.3	(7.0–7.5)	1,997	5.1	(4.8–5.3)	1,241	3.1	(3.0–3.3)
55–64	M	584	4.5	(4.1–4.9)	1,684	13.0	(12.4–13.6)	819	6.3	(5.9–6.8)	664	5.1	(4.7–5.5)
	F	227	1.6	(1.4–1.8)	282	2.0	(1.8–2.3)	385	2.8	(2.5–3.0)	191	1.4	(1.2–1.6)
	Total	811	3.0	(2.8–3.2)	1,966	7.3	(7.0–7.6)	1,204	4.5	(4.2–4.7)	856	3.2	(3.0–3.4)
65–74	M	796	9.4	(8.8–10.1)	1,332	15.8	(14.9–16.6)	549	6.5	(6.0–7.0)	616	7.3	(6.7–7.9)
	F	461	4.5	(4.1–5.0)	167	1.6	(1.4–1.9)	336	3.3	(3.0–3.7)	258	2.5	(2.2–2.9)
	Total	1,256	6.8	(6.4–7.1)	1,500	8.1	(7.7–8.5)	885	4.8	(4.4–5.1)	874	4.7	(4.4–5.0)
75–84	M	1,481	29.2	(27.7–30.7)	1,242	24.5	(23.1–25.8)	467	9.2	(8.4–10.0)	799	15.7	(14.7–16.8)
	F	1,216	16.0	(15.1–16.9)	110	1.4	(1.2–1.7)	341	4.5	(4.0–5.0)	525	6.9	(6.3–7.5)
	Total	2,697	21.3	(20.5–22.1)	1,352	10.7	(10.1–11.2)	808	6.4	(5.9–6.8)	1,324	10.4	(9.9–11.0)
≥85	M	1,048	78.4	(73.7–83.2)	420	31.4	(28.4–34.4)	174	13.0	(11.1–15.0)	523	39.1	(35.8–42.5)
	F	1,376	43.4	(41.1–45.6)	27	0.9	(0.6–1.2)	129	4.1	(3.4–4.8)	593	18.7	(17.2–20.2)
	Total	2,424	53.7	(51.6–55.9)	447	9.9	(9.0–10.8)	303	6.7	(6.0–7.5)	1,115	24.7	(23.3–26.2)
Total	M	5,247	3.7	(3.6–3.8)	15,792	11.2	(11.0–11.4)	11,574	8.2	(8.0–8.3)	6,221	4.4	(4.3–4.5)
	F	3,614	2.5	(2.4–2.6)	2,664	1.8	(1.8–1.9)	5,076	3.5	(3.4–3.6)	2,794	1.9	(1.8–2.0)
	Total	8,861	3.1	(3.0–3.1)	18,456	6.4	(6.3–6.5)	16,650	5.8	(5.7–5.9)	9,015	3.1	(3.1–3.2)

Abbreviations: CI = confidence interval; F = female; M = male.

TABLE 5. Numbers and age-adjusted rates per 100,000 population for fall-related traumatic brain injury deaths, by year and race/ethnicity — United States, 1997–2007

Year	White, non-Hispanic			Black, non-Hispanic			American Indian/ Alaska Native			Hispanic			Other/ Unknown	Total		
	No.	Rate	(95% CI)	No.	Rate	(95% CI)	No.	Rate	(95% CI)	No.	Rate	(95% CI)	No.	No.	Rate	(95% CI)
1997	5,246	2.4	(2.3–2.5)	444	1.8	(1.6–2.0)	48	3.4	(2.4–4.6)	382	2.2	(2.0–2.5)	175	6,295	2.4	(2.3–2.4)
1998	5,590	2.5	(2.5–2.6)	485	1.9	(1.7–2.1)	40	2.7	(1.8–3.8)	430	2.5	(2.2–2.8)	208	6,753	2.5	(2.5–2.6)
1999	6,075	2.7	(2.6–2.8)	555	2.2	(2.0–2.3)	41	2.8	(1.9–3.9)	430	2.5	(2.2–2.8)	208	7,309	2.7	(2.6–2.7)
2000	5,970	2.6	(2.5–2.7)	463	1.8	(1.6–1.9)	50	3.0	(2.2–4.1)	490	2.7	(2.5–3.0)	197	7,170	2.6	(2.5–2.6)
2001	6,695	2.9	(2.8–3.0)	520	2.0	(1.8–2.2)	47	3.1	(2.2–4.2)	480	2.4	(2.1–2.6)	224	7,966	2.8	(2.8–2.9)
2002	7,249	3.1	(3.0–3.2)	510	1.9	(1.8–2.1)	66	4.1	(3.1–5.3)	540	2.6	(2.4–2.9)	290	8,655	3.0	(3.0–3.1)
2003	7,721	3.2	(3.2–3.3)	540	2.0	(1.8–2.2)	71	4.5	(3.4–5.7)	595	2.9	(2.6–3.1)	298	9,225	3.2	(3.1–3.2)
2004	8,657	3.6	(3.5–3.7)	620	2.3	(2.1–2.5)	61	3.3	(2.5–4.4)	600	2.8	(2.5–3.0)	279	10,217	3.4	(3.4–3.5)
2005	9,024	3.7	(3.6–3.8)	612	2.2	(2.1–2.4)	68	3.7	(2.8–4.7)	692	3.1	(2.8–3.3)	347	10,743	3.6	(3.5–3.6)
2006	9,356	3.8	(3.7–3.8)	642	2.3	(2.1–2.5)	77	3.9	(3.1–5.0)	751	3.0	(2.8–3.2)	356	11,182	3.6	(3.6–3.7)
2007	10,178	4.0	(3.9–4.1)	596	2.1	(1.9–2.3)	76	4.2	(3.3–5.3)	748	3.0	(2.7–3.2)	386	11,984	3.8	(3.7–3.9)
Total	81,761	3.2	(3.1–3.2)	5,987	2.0	(2.0–2.1)	645	3.6	(3.3–3.9)	6,138	2.7	(2.7–2.8)	2,968	97,499	3.1	(3.1–3.1)

Abbreviation: CI = confidence interval.

TABLE 6. Numbers and age-adjusted rates per 100,000 population for firearm-related suicide and homicide traumatic brain injury deaths, by year and race/ethnicity — United States, 1997–2007

Year	Type of death	White, non-Hispanic			Black, non-Hispanic			American Indian/ Alaska Native			Hispanic			Other/ Unknown	Total		
		No.	Rate	(95% CI)	No.	Rate	(95% CI)	No.	Rate	(95% CI)	No.	Rate	(95% CI)	No.	No.	Rate	(95% CI)
1997	Suicide	11,980	5.9	(5.8–6.0)	944	2.9	(2.7–3.1)	99	4.7	(3.7–5.7)	693	2.4	(2.2–2.6)	231	13,947	5.1	(5.1–5.2)
	Homicide	1,663	0.8	(0.8–0.9)	2,215	6.1	(5.8–6.3)	37	1.7	(1.2–2.3)	767	2.1	(2.0–2.3)	145	4,827	1.7	(1.7–1.8)
	All	14,225	7.0	(6.9–7.2)	3,320	9.3	(9.0–9.7)	152	7.1	(5.9–8.3)	1,542	4.8	(4.5–5.1)	386	19,625	7.2	(7.1–7.3)
1998	Suicide	11,933	5.8	(5.7–5.9)	862	2.6	(2.4–2.7)	114	5.2	(4.2–6.2)	702	2.5	(2.3–2.7)	228	13,839	5.0	(5.0–5.1)
	Homicide	1,465	0.7	(0.7–0.8)	1,925	5.2	(5.0–5.5)	41	1.8	(1.2–2.4)	713	1.9	(1.8–2.1)	129	4,273	1.5	(1.5–1.6)
	All	13,894	6.8	(6.7–6.9)	2,956	8.3	(8.0–8.6)	169	7.5	(6.3–8.7)	1,501	4.6	(4.3–4.9)	368	18,888	6.8	(6.7–6.9)
1999	Suicide	11,370	5.5	(5.4–5.6)	890	2.6	(2.5–2.8)	96	4.1	(3.3–5.1)	662	2.3	(2.1–2.5)	217	13,235	4.8	(4.7–4.8)
	Homicide	1,355	0.7	(0.7–0.7)	1,727	4.6	(4.4–4.9)	36	1.6	(1.1–2.3)	656	1.7	(1.6–1.9)	108	3,882	1.4	(1.3–1.4)
	All	13,231	6.5	(6.4–6.6)	2,768	7.7	(7.4–8.0)	145	6.3	(5.2–7.3)	1,381	4.2	(3.9–4.4)	333	17,858	6.4	(6.3–6.5)
2000	Suicide	11,400	5.5	(5.4–5.6)	867	2.5	(2.3–2.7)	90	4.0	(3.2–5.0)	678	2.2	(2.0–2.4)	203	13,238	4.7	(4.6–4.8)
	Homicide	1,325	0.7	(0.6–0.7)	1,709	4.6	(4.3–4.8)	28	1.1	(0.7–1.6)	685	1.7	(1.6–1.8)	112	3,859	1.4	(1.3–1.4)
	All	13,152	6.4	(6.3–6.5)	2,678	7.3	(7.1–7.6)	127	5.5	(4.5–6.5)	1,417	4.1	(3.8–4.3)	329	17,703	6.3	(6.2–6.4)
2001	Suicide	11,648	5.6	(5.5–5.7)	843	2.4	(2.3–2.6)	95	4.1	(3.3–5.1)	681	2.1	(1.9–2.3)	198	13,465	4.7	(4.6–4.8)
	Homicide	1,353	0.7	(0.6–0.7)	1,781	4.7	(4.5–4.9)	41	1.7	(1.2–2.3)	721	1.7	(1.5–1.8)	105	4,001	1.4	(1.3–1.4)
	All	13,493	6.5	(6.4–6.6)	2,708	7.3	(7.0–7.6)	143	6.0	(5.0–7.0)	1,483	4.0	(3.7–4.2)	313	18,140	6.3	(6.2–6.4)
2002	Suicide	11,737	5.6	(5.5–5.7)	820	2.4	(2.2–2.5)	109	4.5	(3.6–5.4)	692	2.1	(1.9–2.3)	174	13,532	4.7	(4.6–4.8)
	Homicide	1,328	0.7	(0.6–0.7)	1,783	4.6	(4.4–4.8)	47	1.9	(1.4–2.5)	704	1.6	(1.5–1.7)	128	3,990	1.4	(1.3–1.4)
	All	13,497	6.5	(6.4–6.6)	2,715	7.3	(7.0–7.5)	165	6.7	(5.7–7.8)	1,478	3.9	(3.7–4.1)	313	18,168	6.3	(6.2–6.4)
2003	Suicide	11,882	5.6	(5.5–5.7)	798	2.2	(2.1–2.4)	91	3.8	(3.0–4.6)	699	1.9	(1.8–2.1)	181	13,651	4.7	(4.6–4.7)
	Homicide	1,229	0.6	(0.6–0.6)	1,950	5.0	(4.8–5.2)	47	1.7	(1.3–2.3)	729	1.6	(1.5–1.7)	113	4,068	1.4	(1.3–1.4)
	All	13,537	6.4	(6.3–6.5)	2,851	7.5	(7.2–7.8)	149	5.9	(5.0–6.9)	1,501	3.7	(3.5–3.9)	299	18,337	6.3	(6.2–6.3)
2004	Suicide	11,920	5.6	(5.5–5.7)	805	2.2	(2.1–2.4)	117	4.8	(3.9–5.7)	745	2.0	(1.9–2.2)	183	13,770	4.6	(4.6–4.7)
	Homicide	1,247	0.6	(0.6–0.7)	1,753	4.5	(4.2–4.7)	40	1.5	(1.1–2.1)	723	1.6	(1.4–1.7)	91	3,854	1.3	(1.3–1.3)
	All	13,555	6.4	(6.3–6.5)	2,666	7.0	(6.7–7.2)	168	6.7	(5.7–7.8)	1,519	3.7	(3.5–3.9)	283	18,191	6.1	(6.0–6.2)
2005	Suicide	12,147	5.7	(5.6–5.8)	827	2.3	(2.1–2.4)	120	4.8	(3.9–5.7)	704	1.8	(1.7–2.0)	172	13,970	4.7	(4.6–4.7)
	Homicide	1,174	0.6	(0.6–0.6)	1,929	4.8	(4.6–5.1)	43	1.5	(1.1–2.1)	788	1.7	(1.6–1.8)	121	4,055	1.4	(1.3–1.4)
	All	13,747	6.5	(6.3–6.6)	2,883	7.4	(7.2–7.7)	174	6.8	(5.7–7.8)	1,574	3.7	(3.5–3.9)	308	18,686	6.2	(6.1–6.3)
2006	Suicide	12,023	5.6	(5.5–5.7)	814	2.2	(2.1–2.4)	107	4.2	(3.4–5.1)	679	1.7	(1.6–1.8)	178	13,801	4.5	(4.5–4.6)
	Homicide	1,225	0.6	(0.6–0.6)	2,018	5.0	(4.8–5.2)	43	1.6	(1.2–2.2)	736	1.5	(1.4–1.6)	99	4,121	1.4	(1.3–1.4)
	All	13,624	6.4	(6.2–6.5)	2,948	7.5	(7.2–7.8)	157	6.2	(5.2–7.2)	1,486	3.3	(3.2–3.5)	280	18,495	6.1	(6.0–6.2)
2007	Suicide	12,450	5.7	(5.6–5.8)	813	2.1	(2.0–2.3)	96	3.7	(2.9–4.5)	800	2.0	(1.9–2.2)	206	14,365	4.7	(4.6–4.7)
	Homicide	1,265	0.6	(0.6–0.7)	1,973	4.8	(4.6–5.0)	30	1.1	(0.8–1.6)	745	1.5	(1.4–1.6)	85	4,098	1.4	(1.3–1.4)
	All	14,070	6.5	(6.4–6.6)	2,904	7.2	(7.0–7.5)	132	5.0	(4.1–5.8)	1,627	3.7	(3.5–3.9)	302	19,035	6.2	(6.1–6.3)
Total	Suicide	130,490	5.6	(5.6–5.7)	9,283	2.4	(2.3–2.4)	1,134	4.3	(4.1–4.6)	7,735	2.1	(2.0–2.1)	2,171	150,813	4.7	(4.7–4.8)
	Homicide	14,629	0.7	(0.7–0.7)	20,763	4.9	(4.8–5.0)	433	1.6	(1.4–1.7)	7,967	1.7	(1.6–1.7)	1,236	45,028	1.4	(1.4–1.4)
	All	150,025	6.5	(6.5–6.6)	31,397	7.6	(7.5–7.7)	1,681	6.3	(6.0–6.6)	16,509	3.9	(3.9–4.0)	3,514	203,126	6.4	(6.4–6.4)

Abbreviation: CI = confidence interval.

TABLE 7. Numbers and age-adjusted rates per 100,000 population for motor vehicle–related traumatic brain injury deaths, by year and race/ethnicity — United States, 1997–2007

Year	White, non-Hispanic			Black, non-Hispanic			American Indian/ Alaska Native			Hispanic			Other/ Unknown	Total		
	No.	Rate	(95% CI)	No.	Rate	(95% CI)	No.	Rate	(95% CI)	No.	Rate	(95% CI)	No.	No.	Rate	(95% CI)
1997	12,971	6.7	(6.5–6.8)	2,060	6.2	(5.9–6.4)	272	12.8	(11.2–14.4)	1,685	5.4	(5.1–5.7)	427	17,415	6.4	(6.3–6.5)
1998	12,788	6.5	(6.4–6.7)	2,056	6.0	(5.8–6.3)	277	12.2	(10.7–13.7)	1,715	5.2	(4.9–5.5)	402	17,238	6.2	(6.1–6.3)
1999	12,100	6.2	(6.1–6.3)	2,002	5.8	(5.6–6.1)	282	12.7	(11.2–14.3)	1,700	4.9	(4.6–5.2)	392	16,476	5.9	(5.8–6.0)
2000	12,446	6.3	(6.2–6.5)	1,974	5.6	(5.3–5.9)	303	12.8	(11.3–14.3)	1,896	5.1	(4.8–5.4)	381	17,000	6.0	(5.9–6.1)
2001	12,228	6.2	(6.1–6.3)	1,909	5.3	(5.1–5.6)	303	12.4	(10.9–13.9)	2,025	5.3	(5.1–5.6)	404	16,869	5.9	(5.8–6.0)
2002	12,581	6.3	(6.2–6.5)	1,876	5.2	(4.9–5.4)	326	13.3	(11.8–14.7)	2,133	5.4	(5.2–5.7)	410	17,326	6.0	(5.9–6.1)
2003	11,918	6.0	(5.9–6.1)	1,843	5.1	(4.9–5.4)	291	11.8	(10.4–13.2)	2,162	5.4	(5.1–5.6)	404	16,618	5.7	(5.6–5.8)
2004	11,746	5.9	(5.8–6.0)	1,854	5.1	(4.8–5.3)	263	10.1	(8.9–11.4)	2,068	4.9	(4.7–5.1)	392	16,323	5.5	(5.4–5.6)
2005	11,821	5.9	(5.8–6.0)	1,922	5.2	(5.0–5.4)	273	10.5	(9.2–11.8)	2,214	5.0	(4.8–5.3)	390	16,620	5.6	(5.5–5.7)
2006	11,502	5.7	(5.6–5.8)	1,931	5.1	(4.9–5.3)	257	9.7	(8.5–10.9)	2,189	4.8	(4.6–5.0)	391	16,270	5.4	(5.3–5.5)
2007	10,772	5.3	(5.2–5.4)	1,727	4.5	(4.3–4.7)	249	9.5	(8.3–10.6)	1,957	4.2	(4.0–4.4)	378	15,083	5.0	(4.9–5.0)
Total	132,873	6.1	(6.1–6.1)	21,154	5.4	(5.3–5.4)	3,096	11.5	(11.1–11.9)	21,744	5.0	(5.0–5.1)	4,371	183,238	5.8	(5.7–5.8)

Abbreviation: CI = confidence interval.

TABLE 8. Average annual numbers and rates per 100,000 population for firearm-related traumatic brain injury deaths, by age group, sex, and race/ethnicity — United States, 1997–2007

Age group (yrs)	Sex	White, non-Hispanic			Black, non-Hispanic			American Indian/ Alaska Native			Hispanic			Other/ Unknown	Total		
		No.	Rate	(95% CI)	No.	Rate	(95% CI)	No.	Rate	(95% CI)	No.	Rate	(95% CI)	No.	No.	Rate	(95% CI)
0–4	M	11	0.2	(0.1–0.3)	9	0.6	(0.3–1.1)	—*	—	—	5	0.2	(0.1–0.5)	—	26	0.3	(0.2–0.4)
	F	7	0.1	(0.0–0.3)	7	0.5	(0.2–1.0)	—	—	—	3	0.1	(0.0–0.4)	—	18	0.2	(0.1–0.3)
	Total	18	0.2	(0.1–0.2)	16	0.5	(0.3–0.9)	—	—	—	8	0.2	(0.1–0.4)	—	43	0.2	(0.2–0.3)
5–9	M	13	0.2	(0.1–0.4)	10	0.6	(0.3–1.2)	—	—	—	3	0.2	(0.0–0.5)	—	28	0.3	(0.2–0.4)
	F	10	0.2	(0.1–0.3)	5	0.3	(0.1–0.8)	—	—	—	3	0.2	(0.0–0.5)	—	19	0.2	(0.1–0.3)
	Total	22	0.2	(0.1–0.3)	15	0.5	(0.3–0.8)	—	—	—	6	0.2	(0.1–0.3)	—	47	0.2	(0.2–0.3)
10–14	M	92	1.4	(1.1–1.7)	34	2.1	(1.4–2.9)	2	1.8	(0.2–6.4)	19	1.1	(0.7–1.7)	4	150	1.4	(1.2–1.7)
	F	22	0.4	(0.2–0.5)	11	0.7	(0.3–1.2)	—	—	—	6	0.4	(0.1–0.8)	—	41	0.4	(0.3–0.6)
	Total	114	0.9	(0.7–1.0)	44	1.4	(1.0–1.8)	3	1.3	(0.3–3.9)	25	0.7	(0.5–1.1)	5	191	0.9	(0.8–1.1)
15–19	M	610	9.1	(8.4–9.8)	389	24.8	(22.4–27.3)	21	18.6	(11.5–28.5)	209	12.1	(10.5–13.7)	28	1,257	11.9	(11.3–12.6)
	F	100	1.6	(1.3–1.9)	51	3.3	(2.5–4.4)	3	2.8	(0.6–8.1)	26	1.7	(1.1–2.4)	5	185	1.9	(1.6–2.1)
	Total	709	5.4	(5.0–5.8)	440	14.2	(12.9–15.6)	24	10.8	(6.9–16.1)	235	7.1	(6.2–8.1)	33	1,441	7.0	(6.7–7.4)
20–24	M	912	14.4	(13.5–15.4)	610	43.6	(40.1–47.1)	25	25.2	(16.3–37.2)	291	15.2	(13.4–16.9)	42	1,881	18.4	(17.6–19.3)
	F	133	2.2	(1.8–2.5)	73	5.1	(4.0–6.4)	4	4.2	(1.1–10.7)	31	1.9	(1.3–2.8)	8	249	2.6	(2.2–2.9)
	Total	1,045	8.4	(7.9–8.9)	684	24.2	(22.4–26.0)	29	14.9	(9.9–21.3)	321	9.1	(8.1–10.1)	50	2,129	10.7	(10.2–11.1)
25–34	M	1,626	12.8	(12.2–13.4)	720	28.8	(26.7–30.9)	31	18.3	(12.4–26.0)	362	9.6	(8.6–10.6)	58	2,797	13.8	(13.3–14.3)
	F	314	2.5	(2.2–2.8)	107	3.9	(3.2–4.6)	5	3.0	(1.0–6.9)	46	1.4	(1.1–1.9)	12	485	2.4	(2.2–2.7)
	Total	1,940	7.7	(7.3–8.0)	827	15.8	(14.7–16.8)	36	10.6	(7.4–14.7)	408	5.9	(5.3–6.4)	70	3,282	8.2	(7.9–8.5)
35–44	M	1,992	12.9	(12.4–13.5)	339	13.2	(11.8–14.6)	23	13.3	(8.4–19.9)	193	6.6	(5.7–7.5)	44	2,590	11.7	(11.3–12.2)
	F	457	3.0	(2.7–3.2)	80	2.8	(2.2–3.4)	4	2.2	(0.6–5.6)	37	1.4	(1.0–1.9)	12	590	2.7	(2.4–2.9)
	Total	2,448	8.0	(7.6–8.3)	419	7.7	(6.9–8.4)	27	7.6	(5.0–11.0)	230	4.1	(3.6–4.6)	56	3,181	7.2	(6.9–7.4)
45–54	M	2,061	14.0	(13.4–14.7)	170	8.3	(7.1–9.6)	13	9.0	(4.8–15.5)	109	6.1	(4.9–7.2)	33	2,386	12.3	(11.8–12.8)
	F	416	2.8	(2.5–3.1)	41	1.7	(1.2–2.3)	4	2.6	(0.7–6.5)	20	1.1	(0.7–1.7)	10	491	2.4	(2.2–2.7)
	Total	2,477	8.4	(8.0–8.7)	211	4.8	(4.1–5.4)	17	5.7	(3.3–9.1)	129	3.6	(3.0–4.2)	43	2,877	7.3	(7.0–7.5)
55–64	M	1,519	14.8	(14.0–15.5)	82	7.0	(5.6–8.7)	6	6.9	(2.5–15.1)	53	5.6	(4.2–7.3)	24	1,684	13.0	(12.4–13.6)
	F	257	2.4	(2.1–2.7)	13	0.9	(0.5–1.5)	—	—	—	7	0.7	(0.3–1.4)	4	282	2.0	(1.8–2.3)
	Total	1,776	8.4	(8.0–8.8)	95	3.6	(2.9–4.4)	7	3.9	(1.6–8.0)	60	3.0	(2.3–3.9)	28	1,966	7.3	(7.0–7.6)
65–74	M	1,230	17.8	(16.8–18.8)	50	7.2	(5.3–9.5)	4	9.2	(2.5–23.5)	36	6.9	(4.8–9.5)	13	1,332	15.8	(14.9–16.6)
	F	152	1.9	(1.6–2.2)	8	0.8	(0.4–1.6)	—	—	—	4	0.6	(0.2–1.6)	2	167	1.6	(1.4–1.9)
	Total	1,382	9.2	(8.7–9.7)	58	3.5	(2.6–4.5)	5	5.2	(1.7–12.2)	40	3.4	(2.4–4.6)	15	1,500	8.1	(7.7–8.5)
75–84	M	1,174	27.1	(25.5–28.6)	31	9.0	(6.1–12.7)	2	10.8	(1.3–39.1)	27	11.0	(7.2–16.0)	8	1,242	24.5	(23.1–25.8)
	F	104	1.6	(1.3–1.9)	4	0.7	(0.2–1.7)	—	—	—	—	—	—	—	110	1.4	(1.2–1.7)
	Total	1,278	11.9	(11.2–12.5)	35	3.7	(2.6–5.1)	2	4.4	(0.5–15.8)	28	4.6	(3.1–6.7)	9	1,352	10.7	(10.1–11.2)
≥85	M	401	34.7	(31.3–38.1)	7	8.5	(3.4–17.4)	—	—	—	8	13.0	(5.6–25.6)	2	420	31.4	(28.4–34.4)
	F	25	0.9	(0.6–1.3)	—	—	—	—	—	—	—	—	—	—	27	0.9	(0.6–1.2)
	Total	427	10.9	(9.9–11.9)	8	2.6	(1.1–5.1)	—	—	—	9	4.9	(2.2–9.2)	3	447	9.9	(9.0–10.8)
Total	M	11,640	12.0	(11.7–12.2)	2,451	14.3	(13.8–14.9)	129	11.0	(9.1–12.9)	1,315	6.7	(6.3–7.0)	258	15,792	11.2	(11.0–11.4)
	F	1,996	2.0	(1.9–2.1)	403	2.1	(1.9–2.3)	24	2.0	(1.3–3.0)	184	1.0	(0.8–1.1)	56	2,664	1.8	(1.8–1.9)
	Total	13,636	6.9	(6.7–7.0)	2,853	7.9	(7.7–8.2)	153	6.4	(5.4–7.5)	1,499	3.9	(3.7–4.1)	315	18,456	6.4	(6.3–6.5)

Abbreviations: CI = confidence interval; F = female; M = male.
* Rate suppressed because sample size was <20 for all years combined.

TABLE 9. Average annual numbers and rates per 100,000 population for motor vehicle–related traumatic brain injury deaths, by age group, sex, and race/ethnicity — United States, 1997–2007

Age group (yrs)	Sex	White, non-Hispanic No.	Rate	(95% CI)	Black, non-Hispanic No.	Rate	(95% CI)	American Indian/ Alaska Native No.	Rate	(95% CI)	Hispanic No.	Rate	(95% CI)	Other/ Unknown No.	Total No.	Rate	(95% CI)
0–4	M	117	2.0	(1.6–2.3)	51	3.4	(2.5–4.5)	7	7.0	(2.8–14.4)	56	2.6	(2.0–3.4)	8	239	2.4	(2.1–2.7)
	F	98	1.7	(1.4–2.1)	41	2.8	(2.0–3.8)	5	5.1	(1.7–12.0)	42	2.0	(1.5–2.8)	5	191	2.0	(1.7–2.3)
	Total	215	1.9	(1.6–2.1)	92	3.1	(2.5–3.8)	12	6.1	(3.1–10.6)	99	2.4	(1.9–2.9)	13	430	2.2	(2.0–2.4)
5–9	M	115	1.8	(1.5–2.2)	43	2.7	(2.0–3.6)	3	2.8	(0.6–8.3)	37	1.9	(1.4–2.7)	6	204	2.0	(1.7–2.3)
	F	90	1.5	(1.2–1.9)	29	1.9	(1.3–2.7)	3	2.9	(0.6–8.6)	25	1.4	(0.9–2.0)	4	152	1.5	(1.3–1.8)
	Total	205	1.7	(1.5–1.9)	73	2.3	(1.8–2.9)	7	3.4	(1.4–6.9)	62	1.7	(1.3–2.1)	10	356	1.8	(1.6–2.0)
10–14	M	184	2.8	(2.4–3.2)	48	2.9	(2.2–3.9)	5	4.4	(1.4–10.4)	42	2.4	(1.7–3.2)	6	285	2.7	(2.4–3.0)
	F	127	2.0	(1.7–2.4)	26	1.6	(1.1–2.4)	5	4.6	(1.5–10.7)	25	1.5	(1.0–2.2)	5	188	1.9	(1.6–2.1)
	Total	311	2.4	(2.1–2.7)	74	2.3	(1.8–2.9)	9	4.0	(1.9–7.7)	67	2.0	(1.5–2.5)	11	472	2.3	(2.1–2.5)
15–19	M	1,175	17.5	(16.5–18.5)	158	10.1	(8.5–11.7)	30	26.6	(18.0–38.0)	222	12.8	(11.2–14.5)	33	1,619	15.3	(14.6–16.1)
	F	646	10.1	(9.4–10.9)	62	4.1	(3.1–5.2)	16	14.7	(8.4–23.9)	75	4.8	(3.8–6.0)	19	817	8.2	(7.6–8.8)
	Total	1,821	13.9	(13.3–14.6)	220	7.1	(6.2–8.1)	46	20.8	(15.2–27.7)	297	9.0	(8.0–10.1)	51	2,436	11.9	(11.4–12.3)
20–24	M	1,233	19.5	(18.4–20.6)	200	14.3	(12.3–16.3)	35	35.3	(24.6–49.1)	322	16.8	(15.0–18.7)	38	1,829	17.9	(17.1–18.7)
	F	403	6.6	(5.9–7.2)	61	4.3	(3.3–5.5)	13	13.5	(7.2–23.1)	63	4.0	(3.0–5.1)	17	556	5.7	(5.3–6.2)
	Total	1,637	13.2	(12.5–13.8)	261	9.2	(8.1–10.4)	48	24.6	(18.1–32.6)	385	11.0	(9.9–12.1)	55	2,385	12.0	(11.5–12.5)
25–34	M	1,365	10.7	(10.2–11.3)	291	11.6	(10.3–13.0)	43	25.4	(18.4–34.2)	381	10.1	(9.1–11.1)	44	2,124	10.5	(10.0–10.9)
	F	503	4.0	(3.7–4.4)	83	3.0	(2.4–3.7)	18	10.6	(6.3–16.8)	76	2.4	(1.9–3.0)	23	702	3.5	(3.3–3.8)
	Total	1,868	7.4	(7.1–7.7)	374	7.1	(6.4–7.9)	61	18.0	(13.8–23.1)	457	6.6	(6.0–7.2)	67	2,826	7.1	(6.8–7.3)
35–44	M	1,306	8.5	(8.0–8.9)	239	9.3	(8.1–10.5)	30	17.3	(11.7–24.7)	218	7.4	(6.4–8.4)	33	1,826	8.3	(7.9–8.7)
	F	545	3.5	(3.2–3.8)	82	2.8	(2.2–3.5)	14	7.7	(4.2–12.8)	62	2.3	(1.8–3.0)	19	722	3.3	(3.0–3.5)
	Total	1,851	6.0	(5.7–6.3)	322	5.9	(5.2–6.5)	44	12.4	(9.0–16.6)	280	5.0	(4.4–5.6)	52	2,548	5.8	(5.5–6.0)
45–54	M	1,096	7.5	(7.0–7.9)	179	8.8	(7.5–10.1)	20	13.9	(8.5–21.5)	119	6.6	(5.4–7.8)	26	1,440	7.4	(7.0–7.8)
	F	432	2.9	(2.6–3.2)	63	2.6	(2.0–3.4)	9	5.8	(2.6–10.9)	36	2.0	(1.4–2.8)	18	557	2.8	(2.5–3.0)
	Total	1,528	5.2	(4.9–5.4)	241	5.5	(4.8–6.1)	29	9.7	(6.5–13.9)	155	4.3	(3.6–5.0)	44	1,997	5.1	(4.8–5.3)
55–64	M	639	6.2	(5.7–6.7)	95	8.1	(6.6–9.9)	9	10.4	(4.8–19.8)	56	5.9	(4.5–7.7)	20	819	6.3	(5.9–6.8)
	F	305	2.8	(2.5–3.1)	34	2.3	(1.6–3.3)	5	5.3	(1.7–12.4)	25	2.4	(1.5–3.5)	16	385	2.8	(2.5–3.0)
	Total	944	4.5	(4.2–4.8)	129	4.9	(4.1–5.7)	14	7.8	(4.2–13.0)	81	4.1	(3.2–5.0)	36	1,204	4.5	(4.2–4.7)
65–74	M	445	6.4	(5.8–7.0)	49	7.1	(5.2–9.3)	5	11.5	(3.7–26.7)	35	6.7	(4.7–9.3)	16	549	6.5	(6.0–7.0)
	F	276	3.4	(3.0–3.8)	26	2.7	(1.7–3.9)	3	5.8	(1.2–17.0)	18	2.7	(1.6–4.3)	13	336	3.3	(3.0–3.7)
	Total	720	4.8	(4.4–5.1)	75	4.5	(3.5–5.6)	8	8.4	(3.6–16.5)	53	4.5	(3.4–5.9)	29	885	4.8	(4.4–5.1)
75–84	M	400	9.2	(8.3–10.1)	32	9.3	(6.3–13.1)	2	10.8	(1.3–39.1)	19	7.7	(4.6–12.1)	13	467	9.2	(8.4–10.0)
	F	303	4.7	(4.2–5.2)	17	2.8	(1.6–4.5)	2	7.4	(0.9–26.6)	11	3.1	(1.5–5.5)	8	341	4.5	(4.0–5.0)
	Total	704	6.5	(6.0–7.0)	49	5.1	(3.8–6.8)	4	8.8	(2.4–22.4)	30	5.0	(3.3–7.1)	22	808	6.4	(5.9–6.8)
≥85	M	156	13.5	(11.4–15.6)	9	10.9	(5.0–20.6)	—*	—	—	5	8.1	(2.6–18.9)	4	174	13.0	(11.1–15.0)
	F	118	4.3	(3.5–5.0)	5	2.2	(0.7–5.1)	—	—	—	4	3.2	(0.9–8.3)	2	129	4.1	(3.4–4.8)
	Total	274	7.0	(6.2–7.8)	14	4.5	(2.5–7.6)	—	—	—	8	4.3	(1.9–8.5)	6	303	6.7	(6.0–7.5)
Total	M	8,232	8.5	(8.3–8.6)	1,394	8.2	(7.7–8.6)	189	16.2	(13.9–18.5)	1,512	7.7	(7.3–8.0)	246	11,574	8.2	(8.0–8.3)
	F	3,845	3.8	(3.7–3.9)	529	2.8	(2.6–3.0)	92	7.6	(6.2–9.4)	461	2.5	(2.3–2.7)	149	5,076	3.5	(3.4–3.6)
	Total	12,078	6.1	(6.0–6.2)	1,923	5.4	(5.1–5.6)	281	11.8	(10.4–13.2)	1,973	5.2	(4.9–5.4)	395	16,650	5.8	(5.7–5.9)

Abbreviations: CI = confidence interval; F = female; M = male.
* Rate suppressed because sample size was <20 for all years combined.

TABLE 10. Numbers and age-adjusted rates per 100,000 population for motor vehicle–related traumatic brain injury deaths, by year and category of motor vehicle injury — United States, 1997–2007

| | Motor vehicle injury category | | | | | | | | | | | | | | | | | |
| Year | Motor vehicle occupant | | | Motorcyclist | | | Pedal cyclist | | | Pedestrian | | | Other/Unspecified | | | Total | | |
	No.	Rate	(95% CI)	No.	Rate	(95% CI)	No.	Rate	(95% CI)	No.	Rate	(95% CI)	No.	Rate	(95% CI)	No.	Rate	(95% CI)
1997	10,114	3.7	(3.6–3.8)	719	0.3	(0.2–0.3)	432	0.2	(0.1–0.2)	2,167	0.8	(0.8–0.8)	3,939	1.4	(1.4–1.5)	**17,415**	**6.4**	**(6.3–6.5)**
1998	9,897	3.6	(3.5–3.6)	735	0.3	(0.2–0.3)	400	0.1	(0.1–0.2)	2,129	0.8	(0.7–0.8)	4,029	1.5	(1.4–1.5)	**17,238**	**6.2**	**(6.1–6.3)**
1999	7,514	2.7	(2.6–2.7)	1,013	0.4	(0.3–0.4)	326	0.1	(0.1–0.1)	1,773	0.6	(0.6–0.7)	5,850	2.1	(2.0–2.1)	**16,476**	**5.9**	**(5.8–6.0)**
2000	7,708	2.7	(2.7–2.8)	1,191	0.4	(0.4–0.4)	304	0.1	(0.1–0.1)	1,761	0.6	(0.6–0.7)	6,036	2.1	(2.1–2.2)	**17,000**	**6.0**	**(5.9–6.1)**
2001	7,698	2.7	(2.6–2.7)	1,303	0.5	(0.4–0.5)	294	0.1	(0.1–0.1)	1,819	0.6	(0.6–0.7)	5,755	2.0	(2.0–2.1)	**16,869**	**5.9**	**(5.8–6.0)**
2002	8,456	2.9	(2.9–3.0)	1,400	0.5	(0.5–0.5)	280	0.1	(0.1–0.1)	1,803	0.6	(0.6–0.7)	5,387	1.9	(1.8–1.9)	**17,326**	**6.0**	**(5.9–6.1)**
2003	8,091	2.8	(2.7–2.8)	1,524	0.5	(0.5–0.5)	279	0.1	(0.1–0.1)	1,824	0.6	(0.6–0.7)	4,900	1.7	(1.6–1.7)	**16,618**	**5.7**	**(5.6–5.8)**
2004	7,593	2.6	(2.5–2.6)	1,635	0.6	(0.5–0.6)	312	0.1	(0.1–0.1)	1,654	0.6	(0.5–0.6)	5,129	1.7	(1.7–1.8)	**16,323**	**5.5**	**(5.4–5.6)**
2005	7,462	2.5	(2.4–2.6)	1,716	0.6	(0.5–0.6)	365	0.1	(0.1–0.1)	1,724	0.6	(0.6–0.6)	5,353	1.8	(1.7–1.8)	**16,620**	**5.6**	**(5.5–5.7)**
2006	6,858	2.3	(2.2–2.3)	1,880	0.6	(0.6–0.6)	339	0.1	(0.1–0.1)	1,791	0.6	(0.6–0.6)	5,402	1.8	(1.7–1.8)	**16,270**	**5.4**	**(5.3–5.5)**
2007	6,119	2.0	(2.0–2.1)	1,856	0.6	(0.6–0.6)	241	0.1	(0.1–0.1)	1,626	0.5	(0.5–0.6)	5,241	1.7	(1.7–1.8)	**15,083**	**5.0**	**(4.9–5.0)**
Total	87,510	2.8	(2.7–2.8)	14,972	0.5	(0.5–0.5)	3,572	0.1	(0.1–0.1)	20,071	0.6	(0.6–0.6)	57,021	1.8	(1.8–1.8)	**183,238**	**5.8**	**(5.7–5.8)**

Abbreviation: CI = confidence interval.

TABLE 11. Numbers and age-adjusted rates per 100,000 population for motor vehicle–related traumatic brain injury deaths, by category of motor vehicle injury and race/ethnicity — United States, 1997

| Motor vehicle injury category | White, non-Hispanic | | | Black, non-Hispanic | | | American Indian/ Alaska Native | | | Hispanic | | | Other/ Unknown | Total | | |
	No.	Rate	(95% CI)	No.	Rate	(95% CI)	No.	Rate	(95% CI)	No.	Rate	(95% CI)	No.	No.	Rate	(95% CI)
Occupant	7,566	3.9	(3.8–4.0)	1,067	3.2	(3.0–3.4)	172	7.7	(6.5–8.9)	1,060	3.2	(3.0–3.5)	249	10,114	3.7	(3.6–3.8)
Motorcyclist	617	0.3	(0.3–0.3)	53	0.1	(0.1–0.2)	3	0.1	(0.0–0.4)	40	0.1	(0.1–0.2)	6	719	0.3	(0.2–0.3)
Pedal cyclist	293	0.2	(0.1–0.2)	70	0.2	(0.2–0.2)	1	0.0	(0.0–0.2)	57	0.2	(0.1–0.3)	11	432	0.2	(0.1–0.2)
Pedestrian	1,334	0.7	(0.6–0.7)	402	1.2	(1.1–1.3)	35	1.8	(1.2–2.6)	303	1.2	(1.0–1.3)	93	2,167	0.8	(0.8–0.8)
Other	63	0.0	(0.0–0.0)	6	0.0	(0.0–0.0)	2	0.1	(0.0–0.3)	3	0.0	(0.0–0.0)	1	75	0.0	(0.0–0.0)
Unspecified	3,098	1.6	(1.5–1.6)	462	1.4	(1.3–1.6)	59	3.0	(2.2–4.0)	222	0.7	(0.6–0.8)	67	3,908	1.4	(1.4–1.5)
Total	12,971	6.7	(6.5–6.8)	2,060	6.2	(5.9–6.4)	272	12.8	(11.2–14.4)	1,685	5.4	(5.1–5.7)	427	17,415	6.4	(6.3–6.5)

Abbreviation: CI = confidence interval.

TABLE 12. Numbers and age-adjusted rates per 100,000 population for motor vehicle–related traumatic brain injury deaths, by category of motor vehicle injury and race/ethnicity — United States, 2007

| Motor vehicle injury category | White, non-Hispanic | | | Black, non-Hispanic | | | American Indian/ Alaska Native | | | Hispanic | | | Other/ Unknown | Total | | |
	No.	Rate	(95% CI)	No.	Rate	(95% CI)	No.	Rate	(95% CI)	No.	Rate	(95% CI)	No.	No.	Rate	(95% CI)
Occupant	4,405	2.2	(2.1–2.3)	694	1.8	(1.7–1.9)	107	4.0	(3.2–4.8)	789	1.6	(1.5–1.8)	124	6,119	2.0	(2.0–2.1)
Motorcyclist	1,527	0.7	(0.7–0.8)	149	0.4	(0.3–0.5)	11	0.4	(0.2–0.7)	140	0.3	(0.3–0.4)	29	1,856	0.6	(0.6–0.6)
Pedal cyclist	141	0.1	(0.1–0.1)	42	0.1	(0.1–0.1)	2	0.1	(0.0–0.3)	44	0.1	(0.1–0.2)	12	241	0.1	(0.1–0.1)
Pedestrian	936	0.4	(0.4–0.5)	274	0.7	(0.6–0.8)	34	1.3	(0.9–1.9)	293	0.7	(0.6–0.8)	89	1,626	0.5	(0.5–0.6)
Other/Unspecified	3,763	1.9	(1.8–1.9)	568	1.5	(1.3–1.6)	95	3.6	(2.9–4.5)	691	1.5	(1.4–1.6)	124	5,241	1.7	(1.7–1.8)
Total	10,772	5.3	(5.2–5.4)	1,727	4.5	(4.3–4.7)	249	9.4	(8.3–10.6)	1,957	4.2	(4.0–4.4)	378	15,083	5.0	(4.9–5.0)

Abbreviation: CI = confidence interval.

TABLE 13. Average annual numbers and rates per 100,000 population for fall-related traumatic brain injury deaths, by age group, sex, and race/ethnicity — United States, 1997–2007

Age group (yrs)	Sex	White, non-Hispanic No.	Rate	(95% CI)	Black, non-Hispanic No.	Rate	(95% CI)	American Indian/ Alaska Native No.	Rate	(95% CI)	Hispanic No.	Rate	(95% CI)	Other/ Unknown No.	Total No.	Rate	(95% CI)
0–4	M	12	0.2	(0.1–0.4)	6	0.4	(0.1–0.9)	—*	—	—	6	0.3	(0.1–0.6)	—	27	0.3	(0.2–0.4)
	F	6	0.1	(0.0–0.2)	3	0.2	(0.0–0.6)	—	—	—	2	0.1	(0.0–0.4)	—	12	0.1	(0.1–0.2)
	Total	18	0.2	(0.1–0.2)	9	0.3	(0.1–0.6)	—	—	—	9	0.2	(0.1–0.4)	3	39	0.2	(0.1–0.3)
5–9	M	5	0.1	(0.0–0.2)	—	—	—	—	—	—	—	—	—	—	8	0.1	(0.0–0.2)
	F	3	0.1	(0.0–0.1)	—	—	—	—	—	—	—	—	—	—	5	0.1	(0.0–0.1)
	Total	8	0.1	(0.0–0.1)	2	0.1	(0.0–0.2)	—	—	—	2	0.1	(0.0–0.2)	—	12	0.1	(0.0–0.1)
10–14	M	9	0.1	(0.1–0.3)	—	—	—	—	—	—	—	—	—	—	13	0.1	(0.1–0.2)
	F	3	0.0	(0.0–0.1)	—	—	—	—	—	—	—	—	—	—	4	0.0	(0.0–0.1)
	Total	12	0.1	(0.0–0.2)	—	—	—	—	—	—	—	—	—	—	17	0.1	(0.0–0.1)
15–19	M	41	0.6	(0.4–0.8)	3	0.2	(0.0–0.6)	—	—	—	11	0.6	(0.3–1.1)	2	57	0.5	(0.4–0.7)
	F	10	0.2	(0.1–0.3)	—	—	—	—	—	—	—	—	—	—	12	0.1	(0.1–0.2)
	Total	51	0.4	(0.3–0.5)	4	0.1	(0.0–0.3)	—	—	—	11	0.3	(0.2–0.6)	3	70	0.3	(0.3–0.4)
20–24	M	68	1.1	(0.8–1.4)	7	0.5	(0.2–1.0)	—	—	—	21	1.1	(0.7–1.7)	2	99	1.0	(0.8–1.2)
	F	10	0.2	(0.1–0.3)	—	—	—	—	—	—	—	—	—	—	15	0.2	(0.1–0.3)
	Total	79	0.6	(0.5–0.8)	8	0.3	(0.1–0.6)	—	—	—	23	0.7	(0.4–1.0)	4	115	0.6	(0.5–0.7)
25–34	M	122	1.0	(0.8–1.1)	17	0.7	(0.4–1.1)	3	1.8	(0.4–5.2)	52	1.4	(1.0–1.8)	7	201	1.0	(0.9–1.1)
	F	24	0.2	(0.1–0.3)	4	0.1	(0.0–0.4)	—	—	—	3	0.1	(0.0–0.3)	—	33	0.2	(0.1–0.2)
	Total	146	0.6	(0.5–0.7)	21	0.4	(0.2–0.6)	4	1.2	(0.3–3.0)	54	0.8	(0.6–1.0)	9	234	0.6	(0.5–0.7)
35–44	M	253	1.6	(1.4–1.8)	44	1.7	(1.2–2.3)	7	4.0	(1.6–8.3)	60	2.0	(1.6–2.6)	11	375	1.7	(1.5–1.9)
	F	66	0.4	(0.3–0.5)	10	0.3	(0.2–0.6)	2	1.1	(0.1–3.9)	6	0.2	(0.1–0.5)	2	87	0.4	(0.3–0.5)
	Total	319	1.0	(0.9–1.2)	54	1.0	(0.7–1.3)	9	2.5	(1.2–4.8)	66	1.2	(0.9–1.5)	14	462	1.0	(0.9–1.1)
45–54	M	402	2.7	(2.5–3.0)	74	3.6	(2.9–4.6)	9	6.3	(2.9–11.9)	59	3.3	(2.5–4.2)	16	559	2.9	(2.6–3.1)
	F	133	0.9	(0.7–1.0)	17	0.7	(0.4–1.1)	3	1.9	(0.4–5.6)	10	0.6	(0.3–1.0)	4	166	0.8	(0.7–1.0)
	Total	534	1.8	(1.7–2.0)	91	2.1	(1.7–2.5)	12	4.0	(2.1–7.0)	68	1.9	(1.5–2.4)	19	725	1.8	(1.7–2.0)
55–64	M	441	4.3	(3.9–4.7)	64	5.5	(4.2–7.0)	7	8.1	(3.3–16.7)	52	5.5	(4.1–7.2)	20	584	4.5	(4.1–4.9)
	F	180	1.7	(1.4–1.9)	20	1.4	(0.8–2.1)	2	2.1	(0.3–7.7)	17	1.6	(0.9–2.6)	8	227	1.6	(1.4–1.8)
	Total	620	2.9	(2.7–3.2)	84	3.2	(2.5–3.9)	10	5.5	(2.7–10.2)	69	3.5	(2.7–4.4)	29	811	3.0	(2.8–3.2)
65–74	M	655	9.5	(8.7–10.2)	58	8.3	(6.3–10.8)	5	11.5	(3.7–26.7)	51	9.7	(7.2–12.8)	25	796	9.4	(8.8–10.1)
	F	380	4.7	(4.2–5.1)	33	3.4	(2.3–4.7)	3	5.8	(1.2–17.0)	28	4.3	(2.8–6.2)	17	461	4.5	(4.1–5.0)
	Total	1,036	6.9	(6.5–7.3)	91	5.4	(4.4–6.7)	8	8.4	(3.6–16.5)	79	6.7	(5.3–8.3)	42	1,256	6.8	(6.4–7.1)
75–84	M	1,316	30.3	(28.7–32.0)	56	16.2	(12.3–21.1)	5	27.1	(8.8–63.2)	59	24.0	(18.2–30.9)	44	1,481	29.2	(27.7–30.7)
	F	1,086	16.9	(15.9–17.9)	46	7.5	(5.5–10.1)	4	14.7	(4.0–37.7)	45	12.5	(9.1–16.8)	36	1,216	16.0	(15.1–16.9)
	Total	2,402	22.3	(21.4–23.2)	102	10.7	(8.6–12.8)	9	19.7	(9.0–37.4)	104	17.2	(13.9–20.5)	80	2,697	21.3	(20.5–22.1)
≥85	M	946	82.0	(76.7–87.2)	31	37.5	(25.5–53.2)	2	43.8	(5.3–158.0)	33	53.5	(36.9–75.2)	36	1,048	78.4	(73.7–83.2)
	F	1,262	45.7	(43.2–48.3)	44	19.4	(14.1–26.0)	3	30.1	(6.2–88.0)	37	29.9	(21.1–41.2)	30	1,376	43.4	(41.1–45.6)
	Total	2,208	56.4	(54.1–58.8)	76	24.5	(19.3–30.7)	5	34.4	(11.2–80.3)	70	37.8	(29.5–47.7)	66	2,424	53.7	(51.6–55.9)
Total	M	4,270	4.4	(4.3–4.5)	363	2.1	(1.9–2.3)	41	3.5	(2.5–4.8)	407	2.1	(1.9–2.3)	167	5,247	3.7	(3.6–3.8)
	F	3,162	3.1	(3.0–3.2)	181	1.0	(0.8–1.1)	18	1.5	(0.9–2.4)	151	0.8	(0.7–0.9)	102	3,614	2.5	(2.4–2.6)
	Total	7,432	3.7	(3.7–3.8)	544	1.5	(1.4–1.6)	59	2.5	(1.9–3.2)	557	1.5	(1.3–1.6)	269	8,861	3.1	(3.0–3.1)

Abbreviations: CI = confidence interval; F = female; M = male.
* Rate suppressed because sample size was <20 for all years combined.

TABLE 14. Numbers and age-adjusted rates per 100,000 population for traumatic brain injury deaths, by year and place of death* — United States, 1997–2007

Year	Inpatient			ED/Outpatient			Dead on arrival			Home			Nursing home			Other/Unknown		
	No.	Rate	(95% CI)	No.	Rate	(95% CI)	No.	Rate	(95% CI)	No.	Rate	(95% CI)	No.	Rate	(95% CI)	No.	Rate	(95% CI)
1997	14,437	5.4	(5.3–5.5)	6,694	2.5	(2.4–2.5)	2,752	1.0	(1.0–1.0)	11,508	4.3	(4.2–4.3)	1,764	0.7	(0.6–0.7)	15,308	5.6	(5.5–5.7)
1998	14,616	5.4	(5.3–5.5)	6,542	2.4	(2.3–2.4)	2,436	0.9	(0.8–0.9)	11,450	4.2	(4.1–4.3)	1,936	0.7	(0.7–0.8)	15,526	5.6	(5.5–5.7)
1999	14,832	5.4	(5.3–5.5)	6,527	2.3	(2.3–2.4)	2,298	0.8	(0.8–0.9)	11,199	4.0	(4.0–4.1)	1,984	0.7	(0.7–0.8)	15,101	5.4	(5.3–5.5)
2000	14,011	5.0	(4.9–5.1)	6,226	2.2	(2.1–2.3)	2,221	0.8	(0.8–0.8)	11,123	4.0	(3.9–4.0)	1,661	0.6	(0.6–0.6)	15,438	5.4	(5.4–5.5)
2001	14,874	5.2	(5.2–5.3)	6,532	2.3	(2.2–2.3)	2,033	0.7	(0.7–0.7)	11,539	4.0	(4.0–4.1)	1,834	0.7	(0.6–0.7)	15,948	5.6	(5.5–5.6)
2002	14,721	5.1	(5.0–5.2)	6,462	2.2	(2.2–2.3)	1,846	0.6	(0.6–0.7)	11,635	4.0	(4.0–4.1)	1,654	0.6	(0.5–0.6)	16,366	5.6	(5.6–5.7)
2003	15,085	5.2	(5.1–5.3)	6,216	2.1	(2.1–2.2)	1,791	0.6	(0.6–0.6)	12,001	4.1	(4.0–4.2)	1,707	0.6	(0.6–0.6)	16,083	5.5	(5.4–5.6)
2004	15,436	5.2	(5.1–5.3)	6,351	2.1	(2.1–2.2)	1,521	0.5	(0.5–0.5)	11,980	4.0	(4.0–4.1)	1,755	0.6	(0.6–0.6)	16,107	5.4	(5.4–5.5)
2005	15,959	5.3	(5.2–5.4)	6,568	2.2	(2.1–2.3)	1,487	0.5	(0.5–0.5)	12,254	4.1	(4.0–4.1)	2,105	0.7	(0.7–0.7)	16,533	5.5	(5.5–5.6)
2006	16,054	5.3	(5.2–5.3)	6,228	2.1	(2.0–2.1)	1,468	0.5	(0.5–0.5)	12,234	4.0	(3.9–4.0)	2,244	0.7	(0.7–0.8)	16,237	5.4	(5.3–5.4)
2007	16,464	5.3	(5.2–5.4)	5,853	1.9	(1.9–2.0)	1,242	0.4	(0.4–0.4)	12,569	4.1	(4.0–4.1)	2,479	0.8	(0.7–0.8)	16,109	5.3	(5.2–5.4)
Total	166,489	5.3	(5.2–5.3)	70,199	2.2	(2.2–2.2)	21,095	0.7	(0.7–0.7)	129,492	4.1	(4.1–4.1)	21,123	0.7	(0.7–0.7)	174,756	5.5	(5.5–5.5)

Abbreviations: CI = confidence interval; ED = emergency department.
* Distinct from place of injury.

TABLE 15. Average annual numbers and age-adjusted rates per 100,000 population for traumatic brain injury deaths, by place of death* and race/ethnicity — United States, 1997–2007

Place of death	White, non-Hispanic			Black, non-Hispanic			American Indian/Alaska Native			Hispanic			Other/Unknown	Total		
	No.	Rate	(95% CI)	No.	Rate	(95% CI)	No.	Rate	(95% CI)	No.	Rate	(95% CI)	No.	No.	Rate	(95% CI)
Inpatient	11,408	5.2	(5.1–5.3)	1,778	5.6	(5.3–5.8)	140	6.9	(5.7–8.1)	1,362	4.8	(4.5–5.1)	447	15,135	5.3	(5.2–5.3)
ED/Outpatient	4,251	2.1	(2.0–2.1)	1,137	3.1	(2.9–3.3)	74	3.2	(2.5–4.1)	753	2.0	(1.8–2.2)	167	6,382	2.2	(2.2–2.3)
Dead on arrival	1,375	0.7	(0.6–0.7)	354	1.0	(0.9–1.1)	28	1.2	(0.8–1.8)	125	0.3	(0.3–0.4)	35	1,918	0.7	(0.6–0.7)
Home	9,887	4.6	(4.5–4.7)	975	2.9	(2.7–3.1)	95	4.1	(3.3–5.1)	638	2.1	(1.9–2.2)	177	11,772	4.1	(4.0–4.1)
Nursing home	1,675	0.7	(0.7–0.7)	126	0.5	(0.4–0.6)	13	0.9	(0.5–1.6)	74	0.4	(0.3–0.5)	32	1,920	0.7	(0.6–0.7)
Other	10,940	5.5	(5.4–5.6)	2,279	6.2	(5.9–6.5)	266	10.7	(9.4–12.1)	1,911	4.8	(4.6–5.0)	358	15,753	5.4	(5.4–5.5)
Unknown	96	0.0	(0.0–0.1)	17	0.1	(0.0–0.1)	2	0.0	(0.0–0.2)	11	0.0	(0.0–0.1)	7	134	0.0	(0.0–0.1)
Total	39,632	18.8	(18.6–19.0)	6,667	19.3	(18.8–19.7)	618	27.2	(24.9–29.5)	4,874	14.4	(13.9–14.8)	1,223	53,014	18.4	(18.2–18.5)

Abbreviations: CI = confidence interval; ED = emergency department.
* Distinct from place of injury.

FIGURE 1. Average annual rates for traumatic brain injury deaths, by age group and sex — United States, 1997–2007

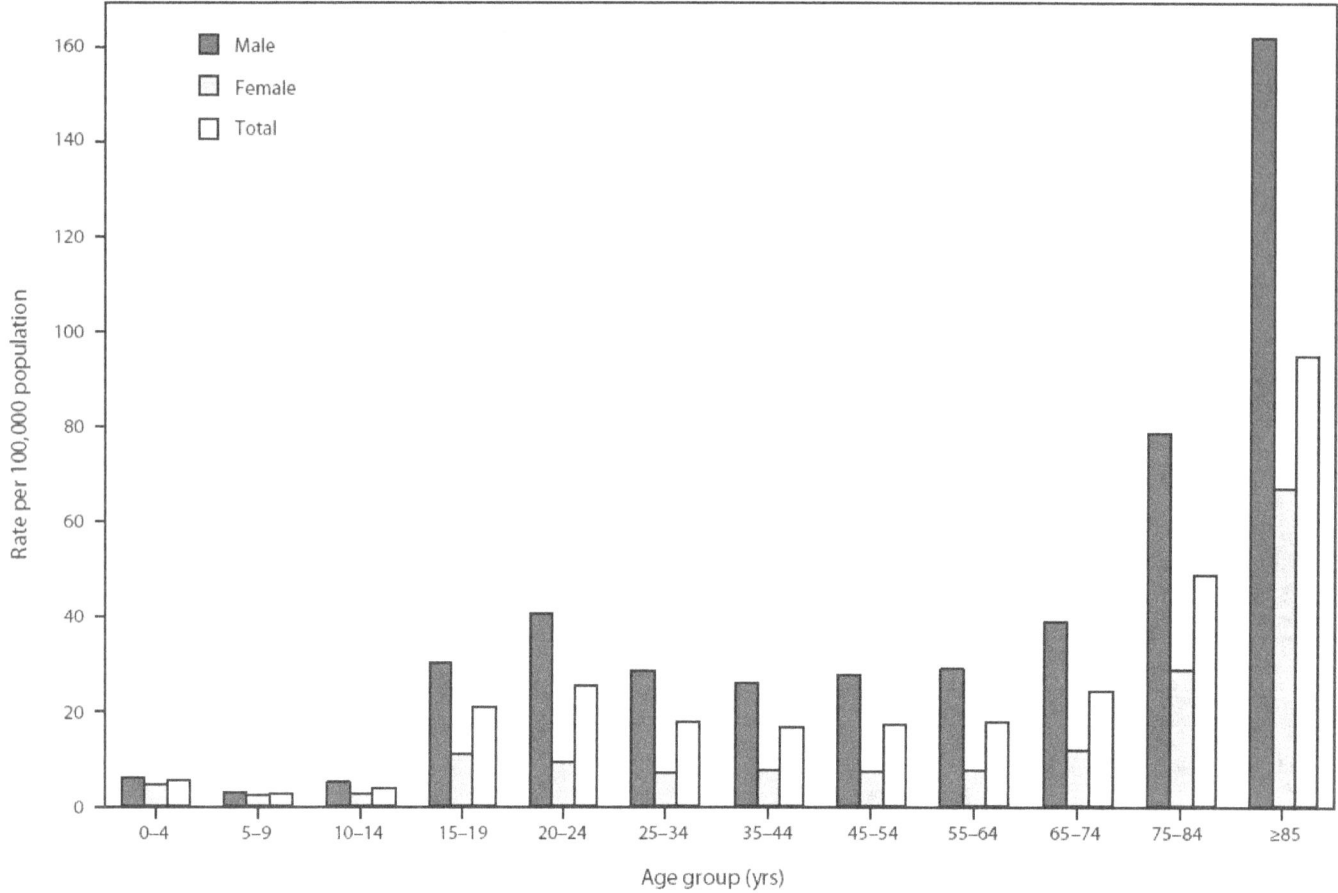

FIGURE 2. Age-adjusted rates for traumatic brain injury deaths, by year and race/ethnicity — United States, 1990–2007

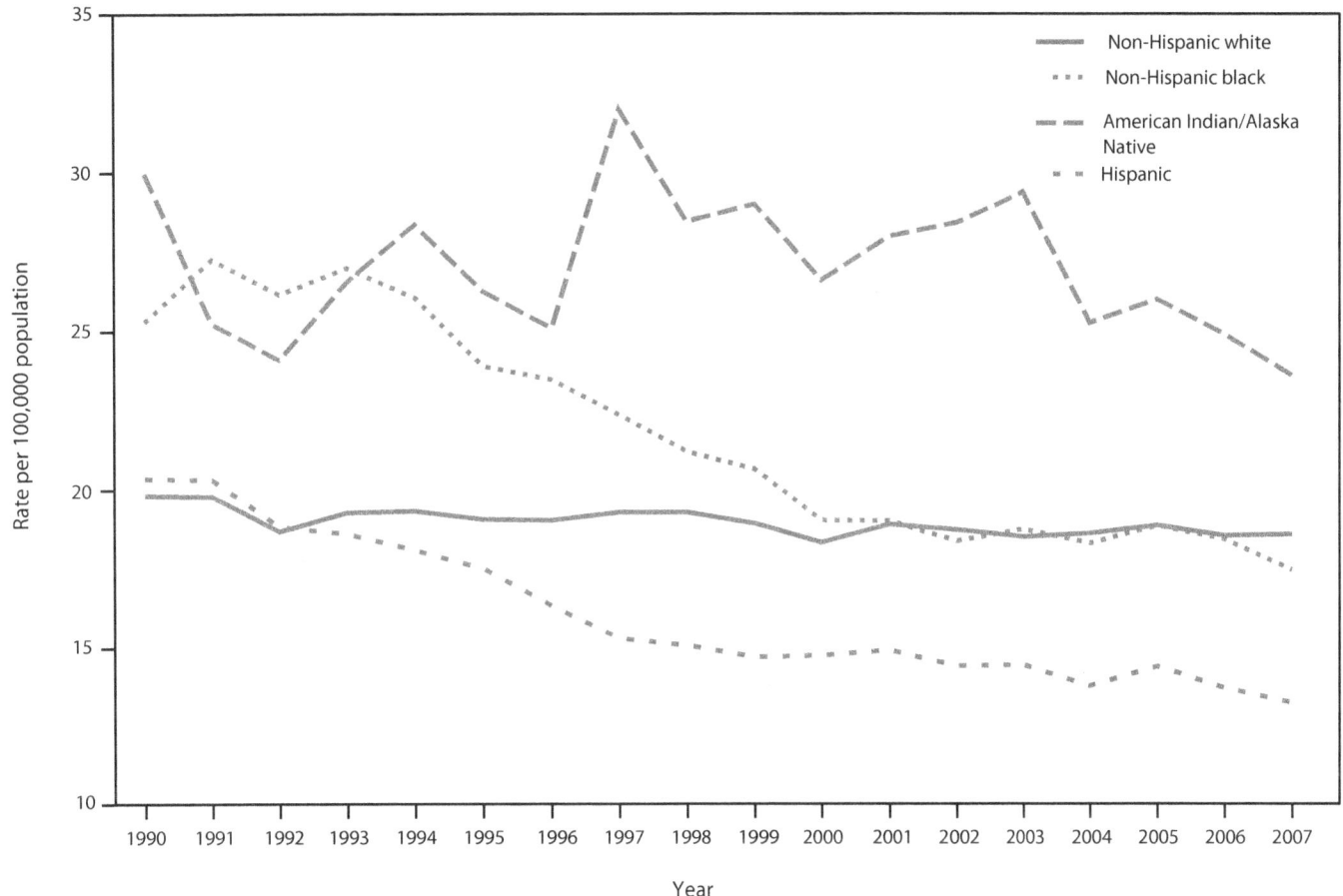

FIGURE 3. Percentage of traumatic brain injury deaths, by race/ethnicity and external mechanism of injury — United States, 1997–2007

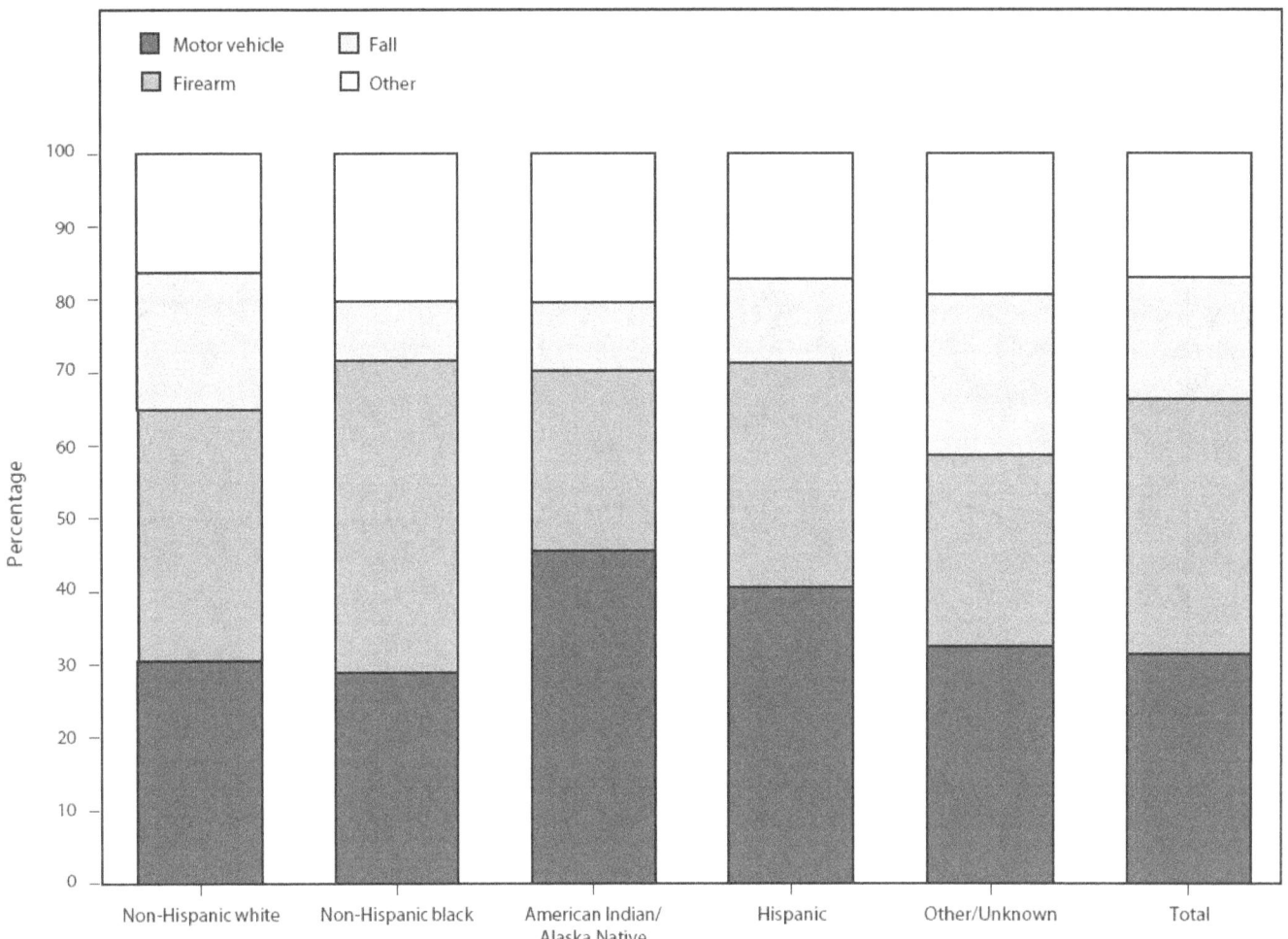

FIGURE 4. Age-adjusted rates for traumatic brain injury deaths, by year and external mechanism of injury — United States, 1990–2007

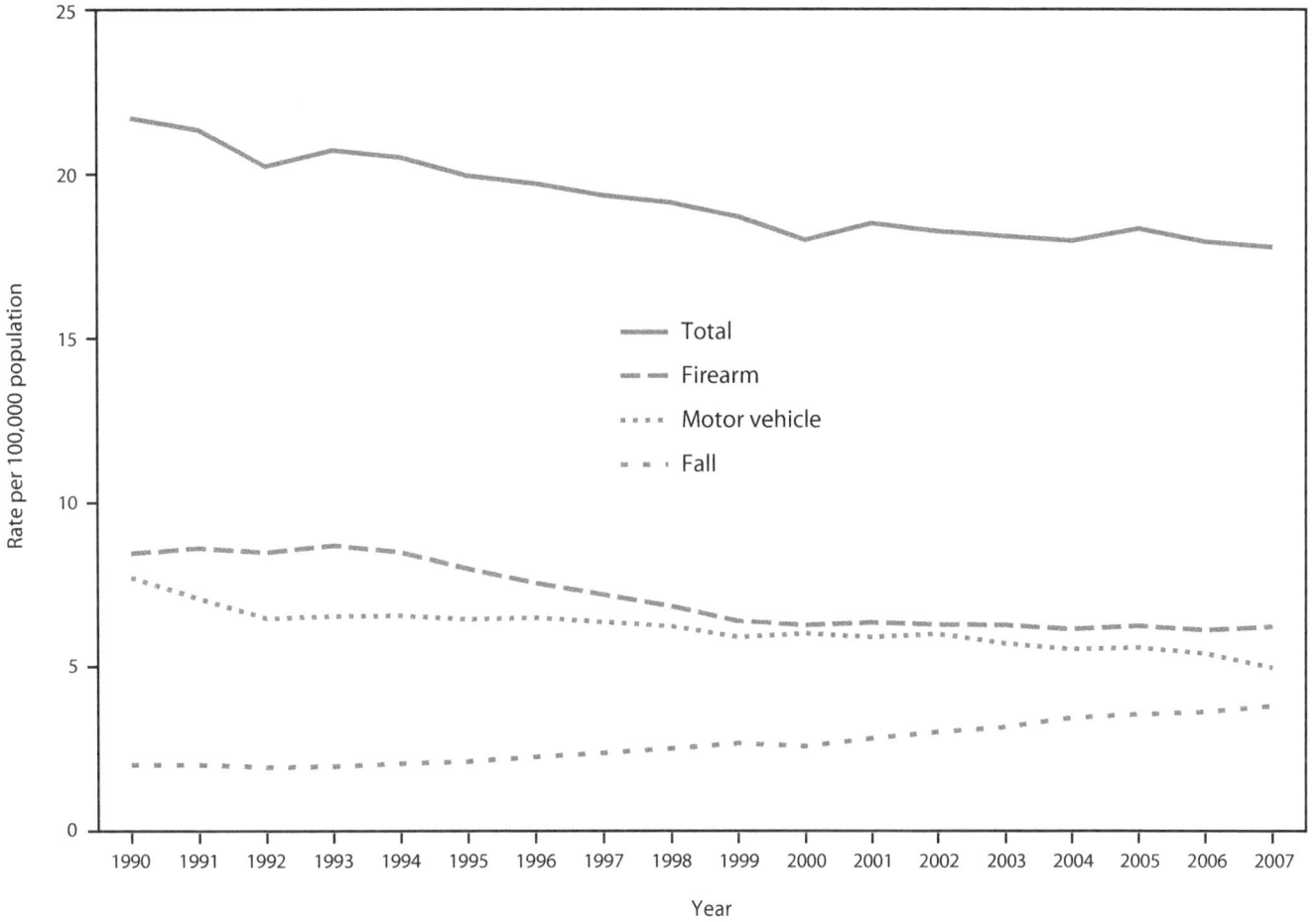

FIGURE 5. Average annual rates for traumatic brain injury deaths, by age group and external mechanism of injury — United States, 1997–2007

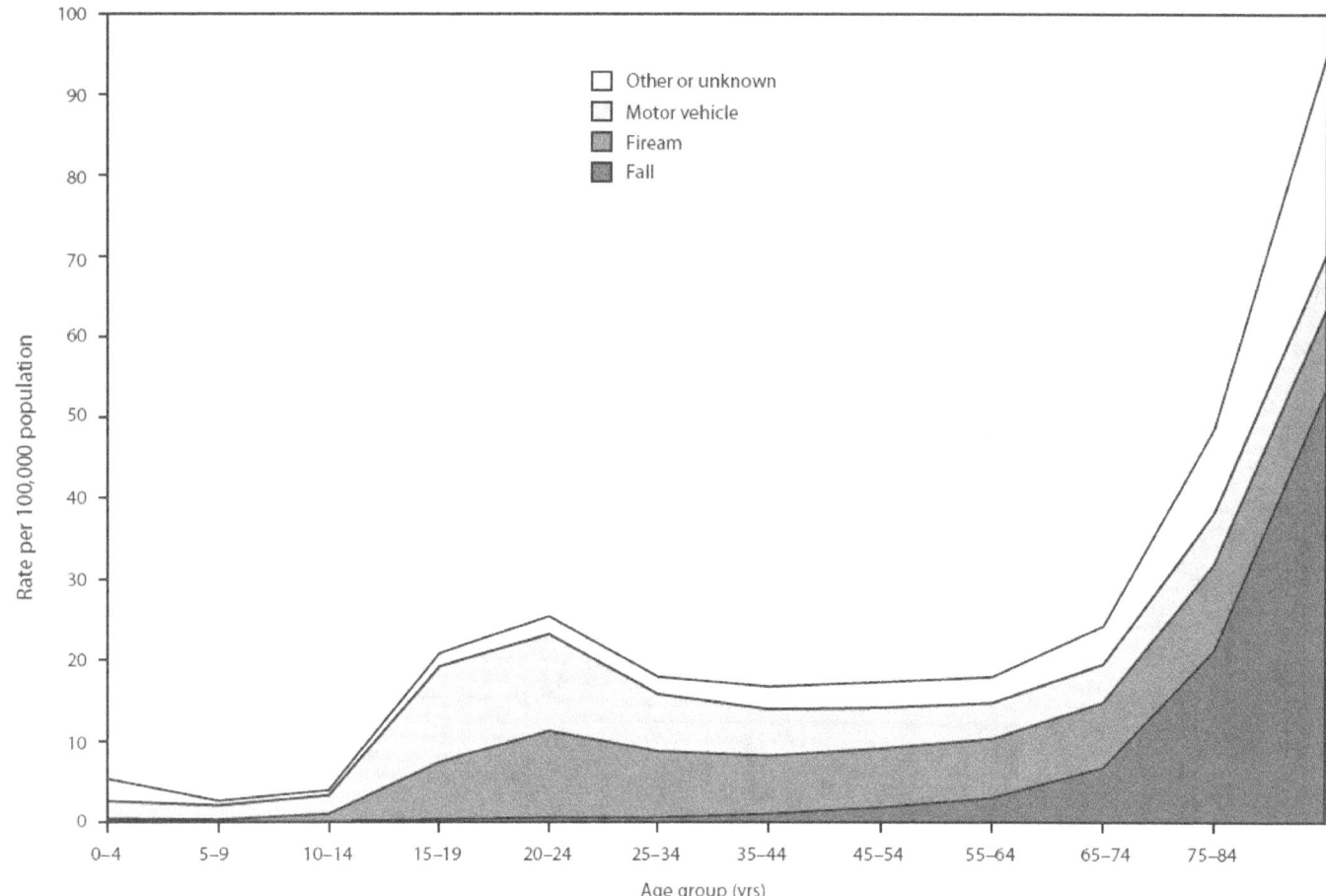